2

SELLING CULTURE

DEBORA SILVERMAN

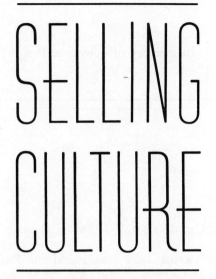

SELLING CULTURE

BLOOMINGDALE'S,

DIANA VREELAND,

AND THE NEW ARISTOCRACY

OF TASTE IN

REAGAN'S AMERICA

PANTHEON BOOKS

NEW YORK

In memory of Theodore Prager

Library of Congress Cataloging-in-Publication Data

Silverman, Debora, 1954–
Selling culture.

Bibliography: p.
Includes index.
1. United States—Popular culture—History—20th century.
2. Fashion—United States.
3. Mass media—United States.
4. Department stores—
Social aspects—United States.   I. Title.
E169.12.S5184   1986   973.927   86-4920
ISBN 0-394-55109-5
ISBN 0-394-74303-2 (pbk.)

Manufactured in the United States of America

Design by Judy Henry

First Edition

PICTURE CREDITS

I am grateful to the following for permission to reproduce the illustrations in this book:

Page 124. Engraving by Chaveau, "Monsieur roy de Perse," Bibliothèque Nationale, Versailles.

Page 127. "Polo" fragrance ad, Vogue, December 1984. Courtesy of Polo/ Ralph Lauren.

Page 133. © Warhol/V.A.G.A., New York 1986.

Page 138. Drawing by David Levine. Reprinted with permission from The New York Review of Books. *Copyright © 1983 Nyrev, Inc.*

Page 153. Copyright © 1985, Jacqueline Cochran, Inc. All rights reserved. Reprinted with permission.

CONTENTS

PREFACE

This book grew out of historical research on the revival of aristocratic cultural traditions in late nineteenth-century France. For
the past five years I have been preparing a book on the fin-de-siècle
French arts and crafts movement, usually associated with the
exuberant organic style called Art Nouveau. In formulating their
modern style, 1890s French artists and craftsmen and their
political sponsors turned to two models: a national aristocratic
design tradition, the rococo, whose organic spatial ensembles were
called in the eighteenth century *style moderne*; and Chinese and
Japanese imperial crafts, whose naturist vocabulary had originally
been incorporated into the eighteenth-century French rococo arts.
Politicians and artists of the 1890s associated these aristocratic design
models with distinctively female qualities, transmitting to the late
nineteenth century a legacy of French modernism as intimate, organic,
and feminine.

As I was compiling and writing this material on the recuperation
of French and Chinese aristocratic crafts in the 1890s, the New York
Metropolitan Museum of Art began a series of shows at its Costume
Institute that were organized by special museum consultant Diana
Vreeland. The first of these shows, which took place in 1980, was
"Costumes of China: The Ch'ing Dynasty." This was followed, in
1981 and 1983, by two French exhibits: "The Eighteenth-Century
Woman" and "La Belle Epoque." Not only were there clear overlaps
in the subjects of my research, but the themes of these Vreeland
shows had striking affinities with themes I was exploring in another
national context: the emphasis on aristocratic and imperial traditions
of luxury craftsmanship; the peculiarly feminine role in the decora-

tive arts, and the role of woman as a decorative object; and the organic, interiorizing opulence of these design models and their link to aristocratic insulation. I became intrigued with a set of questions: Why China and France, and this particular aristocratic image of them, at this particular moment? What was the meaning and significance of a museum celebration of historical examples of social distinction, opulent fashion, and extravagant femininity in the political culture of the 1980s? Who was sponsoring the shows, and what were their attitudes toward their materials?

As I explored these questions, I discovered that the Vreeland shows were part of a broader movement of aristocratic invocation in 1980s American culture, whose participants combined representatives from the worlds of the museum, the department store, fashion design, and the media. At first glance, this group seemed to share, with other elites throughout history, an interest in the selective appropriation of the past to suit present purposes. Historians have analyzed many examples, in Europe and America, of the pursuit of aristocratic revivals—such as Napoleon III's rococo revival—or of the "invention" of royal traditions—such as the creation of national rituals and commemorative ceremonies by the British monarchy after 1850. In each case the appeal to the historical past served to provide a sense of stability and continuity in periods of crisis and dislocation. On closer examination, the 1980s American aristocratic movement is profoundly different from these historical precedents. Other instances of aristocratic revival or invented tradition were marked by a heightened attentiveness to the historical record on the part of their participants; immersion in and reference to the details of the past they were recreating was a prerequisite for the legitimacy of their projects. The 1980s group, by contrast, pursue a fundamentally antihistorical project. As the managers and products of a media culture, they elicit aristocratic material, not as models of historical anchorage, but as novel images for consumer sales. For them, aristocracies are not a diverse elite, specified by their national and historical locations, but an undifferentiated vision of surface luxury, opulence, and dedication to "the good life." The purpose of the 1980s aristocratic movement is not, like that of its predecessors, to create stability amidst change, but to promote the transience, discontinuity, and novelty required by the engines of consumerism. Paradoxically, its appeal to the historical past is pressed into the service of an attack on history and historical consciousness.

The themes and personnel of the 1980s aristocratic movement have direct political meaning and significance. Many prominent figures in the circles of Ronald and Nancy Reagan are important members of this cultural coterie. And the distortion of history so central to the Vreeland museum spectacles resonates deeply with a presidential leadership dedicated to public relations, image making, and the obliteration of the past. While Mrs. Vreeland's practice of being what she calls "terrible on facts," of "always exaggerating," shaped her years of success as a bold and imaginative fashion magazine editor, her exercise of opulent fantasies as art museum historical exhibits is distressing and inappropriate. And Ronald Reagan's "lifelong habit for exaggerating" and his extreme "freedom with facts" have extended the glorification of personal fantasies to a significant force in national life.

I believe that this politics and culture of wish-fulfillment needs to be identified and criticized. This double dose—of museum exhibits recklessly disregarding historical materials, and of political appeals to "dreams come true"—presents powerful corrosive agents to historical thinking. In attempting to hold up to view the debasement of historical consciousness at this particular moment in our political culture, I am aware that the evolution from reality to image is part of a long American tradition. Historians have charted a broad shift, beginning in the 1890s, from the values of production to the values of consumption in American society and personality, in which the roles of image and illusion were catapulted to prominence. Scholars such as Jackson Lears and William Leach have identified the emergence of what Leach has called an "image-saturated" consumer society at the turn of the nineteenth century, and the transition from a Puritan ethic of self-discipline and self-control to a new consumer ethic of self-fulfillment and personal pleasure. Leo Lowenthal and Paul Carter have situated this transformation in the 1920s, when the consolidation of mass entertainment, mass spectator sports, and media exposure transferred national hero-worship from what Lowenthal dubbed "idols of production" to "idols of consumption." The idol of production was inner-directed, aggressive, and driven, admired for his achievements and hard work. The idol of consumption was outer-directed, passive, and lucky, admired for his good looks and for pleasing others. Robert Dallek has connected the gap between image and reality in Ronald Reagan's politics to this shift toward idols of consumption and has traced Reagan's immersion in the values of the modern consumer culture. And political scientist Michael Rogin has deepened this analysis by examining the powerful imprinting of Ronald Reagan's movie roles on his personality and ideology.

I would like this book to be part of the larger historical discussion of the long-term emergence of image and illusion in the culture and politics of American consumer society, and to parallel Dallek's and Rogin's short-term evaluation of Ronald Reagan's "politics of symbolism" by a reading of a specific set of cultural events. I would also like this book to be connected to other analyses of the power of image in American culture by writers such as Richard Schickel and Barbara Goldsmith. Schickel's *Intimate Strangers: The Culture of Celebrity* (1984) and Goldsmith's 1983 article "The Meaning of Celebrity" identify the erosion of ethical standards and the amoral manufacture of celebrity status by the force of American commercial television. Goldsmith in particular suggests how the long-term American preference for illusion has been given new meaning and power in the last twenty years, owing to the combination of technological expansion and the collective disillusionment following the destruction of the heroes of the 1960s—Martin Luther King and the Kennedys—and the Watergate-Vietnam crises. My project has been enriched by these discussions of the appeal of fantasy heroes and the weakening boundaries of self bombarded by absorbing media images; Goldsmith warned in her article that "a society that exalts flights from reality sets a dangerous course." My own treatment suggests the seepage of the values identified by Schickel and Goldsmith in relation to the form and content of television into an arena hitherto considered protected from the onslaught of fantasy: the art museum. And my argument will highlight the theme of the amoral culture of image in the course of an in-depth description of one specific complex of cultural events from the past four years and its particular political kinship with the Reagan-image White House.

I have pursued this project in part because of my disappointment with the waning of critical discourse concerning Reagan the man, his policies, and the social and cultural world that has taken shape around him. This muting of criticism is especially perplexing because of the sheer volume of evidence that can be marshaled to call into question the president's actions, motives, policies, and quality of mind. Anthony Lewis of the *New York Times* has relentlessly and lucidly provided his readers with a consistent account of Reagan's "corruption of language" and "distortion of history" and the startling record of immorality among scores of top Reagan advisers. Yet Lewis's and many other journalists' voices seem to lack reverberation; the buoyant image of an always cheerful, earnest, reassuring, and ageless actor on television saps our resolve to keep complex reality and simple wish sorted out in a sober fashion. An extreme example of this public worship of the Reagans appeared in the June 1985 issue of *Vanity Fair* magazine, for which Ronald and Nancy Reagan, dressed to the nines before a state dinner for the Argentine president, agreed to pose. The exclusive photo series shows the couple dancing, embracing, and caught in a close-up intimate kiss. Intellectual conservative William F. Buckley wrote two pages of tribute to the Reagans' love as they danced around his words. Buckley, usually a rigorous thinker, let strange analogies fly for this occasion, comparing the couple to royalty the world over, and to Baucis and Philemon, associating Nancy's face with the face of the Pietà, and likening Ron to a "baroque" spinner of tales who runs rings around his intelligent listeners. Buckley went on to compare the amorous devotion of the Reagans to that of Whittaker Chambers and his wife, Esther. Chambers, who was posthumously awarded the Medal of Freedom by President Reagan, would surely have been included in Roy Cohn's guest list for his annual birthday party, co-hosted last year by the Reagans and Diana Vreeland at the New York club the Palladium.

Now that we have entered the second half of Reagan's second term, we can look back at the events and symbolic acts of the first years of the Reagan presidency, and the cultural impulses it encouraged, with a historical perspective. In other periods of American history, we could imagine a Mark Twain, an H. L. Mencken, or a Thorstein Veblen going to work, in their distinctive modes, with such material. We need now to have such reckonings applied to figures drawn so bewilderingly out of scale.

· · ·

This book is not intended as a definitive or exhaustive project, but as a discrete cultural reading to stimulate thought and discussion, to isolate themes and issues that have risen to prominence in the New York museum world and the Washington political center since 1980. There are surely strong countercurrents to the aristocratizing impulse I have emphasized here, both in continuing American historical legacies of republican virtue and simplicity and in contemporary fashions for minimalism, punk rock, and the *sportif* casual L. L. Bean. My intention is to characterize the aristocratic strain as it appeared in high culture and consumerism, and to situate it in relation to a particular political program and outlook. Nor do I wish this work to be misunderstood as a challenge to the role of costume or fashion in the art museum. Costume has provided, in the Smithsonian Museum, the Los Angeles County Museum, and the Paris Musée de la Mode, for example, a unique and invaluable way to understand aspects of the history of society and culture. The Smithsonian's 1974 exhibition, "Suiting Everyone: The Democratization of Clothing in America," and the 1983 Los Angeles show, "The Eighteenth Century: An Elegant Art," were models of historical interpretation, public education, and technical perfection. It is the mistreatment of history and the public in Mrs. Vreeland's costume shows and their blatant connection to the immediate needs of fashion merchandising that make them, I believe, objectionable, and misplaced as museum presentations. It is true that museum staffs now face the pressure of corporate sponsorship and the need to find nongovernment funds; but curators and historians have, and will find, better ways to adjust to the new patrons than Vreeland's distortion of costume history for commercial fashion advertising.

Many people have helped me with this book and have contributed time, support, and ideas at crucial stages of the project. While not responsible for this work, my teachers Carl Schorske, Jerrold Seigel, Arno Mayer, and Natalie Zemon Davis provided, each in his or her distinctive way, important models of inspiration by their commitment to relating historical scholarship, morality, and politics. I am indebted to Temma Kaplan and Lizabeth Cohen, who encouraged me to pursue this research at a crucial early stage. Their advice, ideas, and energies enabled me to begin and to finish the book. I am indebted to Michael Walzer, Clifford Geertz, Eve Silverman, Michael Rogin, and Linda Nochlin, who offered readings, suggestions, and generous assistance in placing the manuscript as it neared completion. Many friends and colleagues read the manuscript at different points and were helpful in various ways that I cannot detail here but deeply appreciate: Robert Dallek, Tom Hines, Delores Hayden, Sherrill Cohen, David Biale, Margaret Rustin, Michael Rustin, Joyce Appelby, Bert Hansen, Rachel Klein, Robert Burr, Liz Burr, Sarah Maza, Robert Westman, Deborah Nord, Philip Nord, Dina Copelman, Mel Pollner, Judy Pollner, Jeff Alexander, Ruth Bloch, Ann Koblitz, Lee Bienen, Leonard Wallock, Ed Berenson, Catherine Johnson, Herrick Chapman, Leila Kinney, Paul Summit, Mary McLoed, Mark Phillips, Ruth Phillips, Barbara Schneider, Abbie Phillips, Robert Darnton, Jackson Lears, Albert Boime, Susan Stuard, Eliot Shore, Jeff Weinstein, Geoffrey Gilbert-Hamerling, Michael Hui, and Stephen Boliver.

I would like to thank Lucille Allsen, Lynda Emery, and Peg Clarke for their expert and patient typing of parts of the manuscript, their stylistic improvements, and valuable reactions.

I am very fortunate to have been able to work with André Schiffrin and Sara Bershtel of Pantheon Books. Their critical comments and suggestions enabled me to expand and rethink parts of the manuscript as it was revised for publication. The book would never have reached production without the expert and tireless attention of Carolyn Marsh, to whom I am especially grateful.

Finally, I would like to thank my parents, David and Ziona Silverman, who read and commented on the manuscript, and are constantly sustaining. My debt to my husband, Jeffrey Prager, extends far beyond the bounds of this project, but his ideas, comments, and suggestions indelibly shaped the manuscript. It is in remembrance of his father, Theodore Prager, a man who committed his life to a vision of social justice, that I dedicate the book.

SELLING CULTURE

INTRODUCTION

A woman should look like a woman. . . . I'm tired of jeans and long hair.
— Nancy Reagan, 1980

Everything is power and money and how to use them both. . . . We musn't be afraid of snobbism and luxury.
— Diana Vreeland, 1980

In the year preceding the 1984 presidential election, one million people viewed a lavish exhibition at the Metropolitan Museum of Art in New York: a retrospective entitled "Twenty-five Years of Yves Saint Laurent." Organized by Diana Vreeland, editor for over thirty years at *Harper's Bazaar* and *Vogue* and now special consultant to the Met's Costume Institute, the Saint Laurent show celebrated the "genius" of "haute couture." Galleries filled with mannequins in gilded tunics, embroidered ball gowns, and flowing cocktail dresses were presented to the public as exceptional works of art, divested of all commercial imperatives. Vreeland glorified Saint Laurent as the "dauphin," the rightful inheritor of the noble craft of the couturier, whose sumptuous creations originally graced the forms of French queens and aristocrats. The Met exhibit was a tribute not only to the visionary designer but also to his illustrious customers, whose names, as lenders of the lavish outfits, were inscribed on labels in front of each clothing display. As Saint Laurent was hailed as the scion of the great aristocratic French dressers, so too were his affluent clients touted as the natural successors to the Old Regime elites.

Visitors to the Saint Laurent show found the museum exhibition curiously indistinguishable from the same designer's displays at fashionable department stores such as Bloomingdale's and Neiman-

---

3

Saint Laurent evening wear at the Met

Marcus. The galleries at the Met were not organized according to a chronological development, befitting an artist's "retrospective." Nor did the show instruct us about the way Saint Laurent's opulent ensembles were actually made, or about the position of these haute couture productions within the complex YSL fashion empire devoted to designer mass marketing. Instead the galleries were arranged by color schemes, and by the "timeless" divisions that structure a certain type of woman's day: "day-wear" suits for strolling and shopping; "cocktail hour" dresses in black and white; and lavish "evening clothes" from ball gowns to ruffled "gazar" capes. Vreeland's Saint Laurent show succeeded, not as museum education, but as a giant advertising campaign for French haute couture, as a public testimonial to the loyal patrons of the "dauphin" of fashion, and as a glorification of woman as an objet d'art, for whom life is an interminable round of changing from one luxurious outfit to another.

The triumph of French distinction, opulent fashion, and extravagant femininity in the Metropolitan Museum of Art in 1984 was not an isolated or an accidental phenomenon. Indeed, the Saint Laurent show was part of an important movement of aristocratic posturing in American culture and politics. The movement is centered in New York, with direct links, in both personnel and themes, to the center of political power in the White House of Ronald and Nancy Reagan. Though the movement originated before Reagan's arrival, the 1981 inauguration of a president dedicated to visible wealth and an unchecked "new luxury" solidified its ranks and gave it political meaning and significance.

The affiliates of the aristocratic movement span the worlds of politics, the media, fashion design, the department store, and the museum. Their aristocratic self-image and group identity are perpetuated by Reagan's economic policies, which benefit a small minority and distance them more and more from the majority of Americans. At the center of the aristocratic movement is a fundamental contradiction typical of Reaganism. While styling themselves an exclusive elite of wealth and cultivation, the aspirants to a new American nobility are dependent for their success and values upon the mass market and leveling consumerism.

A gala party launching the Saint Laurent exhibit at the Metropolitan Museum offered a group portrait of this amalgamated elite.

Yves Saint Laurent gala at the Met, December 5, 1983
(Thomas Iannaccone/W)

Diana Vreeland and Yves Saint Laurent
(Thomas Iannaccone/W)

On December 5, 1983, eight hundred guests paid $500 each to dine and dance in the Met's main hall in honor of the Saint Laurent show's opening. For the evening's festivities, Saint Laurent's fabric supplier, Gustav Zumsteg, swathed the main hall in fifteen thousand yards of fuchsia and orange silk. The dinner alone cost $80,000; the total cost for the event was underwritten by Saint Laurent's perfume licensee, Charles of the Ritz. With few exceptions, the distinguished female guests arrived in Saint Laurent evening dresses and seemed like live counterparts of the YSL mannequins arrayed in the galleries below. Nancy Kissinger, sheathed in a black Saint Laurent ensemble with glittering jewel trim, arrived with Henry; others from the world of politics included Evangeline Bruce, widow of the ambassador and dowager of Washington social circles; Mercedes Kellogg, whose husband was a recent Reagan ambassadorial appointee; Houston socialite Lynn Wyatt, wife of Oscar, a major Reagan contributor; and Pat Buckley, who was the social chairperson responsible for organizing the entire evening. Media celebrities attending the gala included Bill Paley, chairman of CBS; Linda Grey of "Dallas"; and Carol Burnett. Fashion designers also came to celebrate Saint Laurent's triumphal entry to the Met: Bill Blass, Oscar de la Renta, Jacqueline de Ribes, and Carolina Herrera. Department-store heads included the chairman of Saks Fifth Avenue. Marvin Traub, the chairman of Bloomingdale's, was unable to attend the party, though he served as an adviser to the Met. Betsy Bloomingdale, out of town, sent her close friend and confidant Jerome Zipkin, the real estate heir who is also a frequent guest and close friend of Nancy Reagan's.

The peculiar combination of fashion, politics, high culture, and consumerism visible at the Met's Saint Laurent show suggested something about the essential qualities of Reaganite political culture. The same group of people featured at the 1983 Met Saint Laurent gala had had their photos splashed across the pages of *Interview* magazine and the *Washington Post* as they flocked, in splendid designer costumes, to the opulent presidential inaugural festivities of 1981. Designer Bill Blass sat in the Reagans' own box at one Kennedy Center inaugural party, where he could survey Nancy's friends Betsy Bloomingdale, Mary Jane Wick, and Estée Lauder shimmering in his signed creations. The Kissingers, Buckleys, de Borchgraves, Wyatts, and Bill Paley were also prominent personages at the Reagan galas, where they joined the Reagans' inner circle of longtime California friends—the Deutsches, Annenbergs, Tuttles, Wicks, Smiths, Jorgensons, Bloomingdales, and Stewarts—in an inaugural extravagance unparalleled in American history. Nancy's wardrobe alone cost $25,000; the cost of an entire week of brunches, lunches, and balls totaled close to $16 million.

Before and after the 1980 elections, the aristocratic tendency was detectable in two centers, whose promoters and ideology were inextricably interrelated. One center was consumerist, spearheaded at Bloomingdale's, where two major marketing campaigns of aristocratic themes were staged. In 1980 Bloomingdale's concentrated on the exotic riches of Chinese emperors, and then turned, in 1983, to the aristocratic crafts of France's Old Regime. The second center of aristocratization was within a bastion of elite culture, the Metropolitan Museum of Art. Under the spell of Diana Vreeland, the Met's Costume Institute offered four exhibitions after 1980 whose subject and forms glorified the luxurious refinements of aristocratic traditions. Translating into high culture the Bloomingdale's sales campaigns, the Met devoted 1980 to "Chinese Imperial Robes," which displayed the palace garb and palace furniture of the Ch'ing dynasty (1644–1912). In 1981 Vreeland shifted to France, staging a celebration of decorative, aristocratic femininity: "The Eighteenth-Century Woman." In 1982 she organized a tribute to the last hurrah of aristocratic womanhood: "La Belle Epoque." Next, in 1983, came a vision of the modern successors to elite female ostentation: "Twenty-Five Years of Yves Saint Laurent." In 1984 Vreeland glorified English gentry and equestrian apparel and ownership in "Man and the Horse," presented by Polo / Ralph Lauren.

The significance of these twin centers of aristocratic invocation, and the national and historical illusions they promote, extends beyond the confines of culture and consumerism to a consideration of its political meaning and resonance. Vreeland's projects glorifying social distinction and female decoration coincide with the reign of a political First Lady devoted to a new luxury, a woman whose passion in life, according to Laurence Leamer, is collecting exclusive designer clothes and never wearing the same ensemble twice. Nancy Reagan's aggres-

Diana Vreeland in her Park Avenue apartment
(Priscilla Rattazzi)

sive amassing of china tableware, White House jewel collections, and twelve double closets full of designer regalia has its advocate in Diana Vreeland, who once claimed that "we mustn't be afraid of snobbism and luxury." Nancy Reagan invited Mrs. Vreeland to dine at the White House, and she shares her passion for the color red—what Vreeland has called "the great clarifier." Her preferred social circle of socialites and fashion designers—including Jerry Zipkin, Betsy Bloomingdale, James Galanos, and Bill Blass—also comprises the social world that Vreeland inhabits.

Yet the conjuncture between politics and the aristocratic cultural movement transcended these individual personalities and social influences. There was a deeper correspondence between the political program of the Reagan White House and the emergence of an aristocratic consumer culture at Bloomingdale's and the Metropolitan Museum. The idealization of non-American nobilities provided the elements of a new cultural style concordant with the politics born at the first Reagan inauguration: a style aggressively dedicated to the cult of visible wealth and distinction, and to the illusion that they were well earned; a style that adopted the artifacts of Chinese emperors, French aristocrats, and English noblemen as signs of exclusivity and renunciation; a style of unabashed opulence, whose mixture of hedonism, spitefulness, and social repudiation was captured in the slogan "Living well is the best revenge." The cast of characters sponsoring the Vreeland and Bloomingdale's spectacles is composed of corporate fashion designers, rich socialites, and mass-media moguls, who constitute a consumerist power elite, the new Reagan elite. The cultural projects they participate in are tied to the big business of illusion making and are perfectly suited to the politics of theater practiced in the White House. Reagan's politics and the aristocratic fashion culture share a fundamental inauthenticity, a reliance on fabrication, and a glaring disparity between symbolism and reality.

. . .

Do Not Cut Out White
Area Between Figures

Inaugural-ball gown of white satin,
overlaid with elaborately beaded lace
in a fern design

A New Gilded Age? From Custodians of Culture to Cultural Cannibals

> *Unsure of themselves, Americans copy*
> *European examples, which bear the guarantee*
> *of long traditions. In spite of a proclaimed*
> *disdain for vulgar prejudice, what constitutes*
> *Society remains in a perpetual thrall to*
> *European fashions. And this is especially true*
> *of external glitter, when the issue is one of*
> *social status and impressing others.*
> — S. Bing, *Artistic America*, 1895

Throughout its history America has always forged an uneasy balance between democracy and luxury, between the ideal of political equality and the fact of economic difference. And, lacking a long history and tradition, affluent Americans have always looked to Europe and beyond for a surrogate lineage through cultural display. The American past is marked by repeated incursions into the treasure troves of European material culture; the architecture, interior design, crafts, and visual arts originally created for European royalty and aristocracy have often been imported to serve as the status badges of the American rich. Isabella Gardner acquired entire sections of Italian ducal palaces and had them reassembled in Boston as her own home; the vast Hoentschel collection of French eighteenth-century rococo furniture and objets d'art was bought by the Wrightsman family and used as their domestic interiors; by transporting lavish materials from the original site, John Paul Getty re-created a perfect replica of the Roman noble Villa Papyri at Herculaneum.

How is the Reaganite aristocratic movement different from other such episodes in American history? Is the contemporary dedication to external riches merely another instance of what Thorstein Veblen called conspicuous consumption? The answers to these questions emerge from the exploration of two fundamental issues. One is the relationship between aristocratic emulation and the obligations of wealth. The second is the relationship between conspicuous consumption, culture, and the historical past, with particular reference to the meaning and function of the art museum.

Thorstein Veblen coined the phrase "conspicuous consumption" to characterize the visible displays of luxury by late nineteenth-century wealthy Americans. Historians have identified this period from 1870 to 1900 as the "Gilded Age," which has some striking parallels to our own "fin de siècle." The post–Civil War decades witnessed a sudden explosion of wealth and the amassing of large private fortunes whose main beneficiaries, the directors of new, large corporations, were branded "Robber Barons" by their critics. With the expiration of the inheritance tax in 1870, the abandonment of the income tax in 1872, and the failure of the 1890 Sherman Anti-Trust Act to offset monopolistic practices, the "new tycoons" like the Rockefellers, Carnegies, Morgans, and Vanderbilts were able to garner profits averaging $800 million in 1892. The staggering increase in some personal incomes was accompanied by a rapid decline in the standard of living among other groups, especially urban workers and new immigrants. The glaring gap between the very rich and the very poor led historian H. Wayne Morgan to describe the Gilded Age as

> an age of extremes—of low wages and huge dividends, of garish display and of poverty, of opulent richness in one row of houses and of degrading poverty a block away. Socially the gap between the haves and the have-nots was greater than our generation would recognize. Who can forget the huge balls and parties thrown by the gentry, and who can visit Newport, Saratoga Springs or Greenbriar without staring in awe at the "cottages" and hostelries built to house the idle rich?

The Robber Barons were scathingly denounced in their own time. American patricians like Henry Cabot Lodge and Charles and Henry Adams chastised the rapaciousness of the "gigantic modern plutocracy and its lawless ways," while Edith Wharton indicted what she called the "monstrous vulgarity" and "varnished barbarism" of the new industrial entrepreneurs' cultural and architectural style, exposing their inability to distinguish between overloaded surface garishness and the necessity for refined "good breeding" in all aspects of "the civilized way of life" among the upper classes. Resonant voices from below— from labor radicals to Populist politicians—also lambasted the Robber Barons. The 1892 Populist platform stated that "the fruits of the toil of millions are boldly stolen to build up colossal fortunes for a few, unprecedented in the history of mankind; and the possessors of these, in turn, despise the Republic and endanger liberty."

American historians have described the variety of manipulative economic strategies the Robber Barons practiced in order to consolidate their gigantic fortunes, often in reckless disregard for the law. John Tipple, for example, noted that they "were correctly identified as destroyers," combining "stock manipulation" and "corporate maneuvering" to "willfully exert prodigious force for their own private benefit, regardless of the consequence to the nation or its ideals." Yet, while acknowledging these excesses of the super rich in the Gilded Age, historians have also emphasized the major positive contributions of the generation of the Robber Barons, particularly in the realm of culture and social philanthropy.

Neil Harris has reminded us that "it is to that supposedly gaudy and giddy era known as the Gilded Age that we owe many of our great cultural institutions, the world-famous opera houses, symphony orchestras and museums that bear the names of America's great cities: New York, Philadelphia, Chicago, and Boston." The massive funding of educational and cultural projects in the 1880s and 1890s cannot be explained by tax incentives or purely economic instrumental goals. The motives instead are linked to ethos and value systems: the Gilded Age elite, however corrupt and rapacious, adhered to assumptions of moral duty, conscience, and the obligations of wealth. Andrew Carnegie's classic apologia, *The Gospel of Wealth*, still retained echoes of the Social Gospel; to the celebration of competitive individualism and the Darwinian struggle won by the rich he added an acknowledgment of the need to legitimize great wealth through public works. Thorstein Veblen characterized the importance of these expressions of "civic virtue" among the Gilded Age American rich: his elite struck a moral bargain with the public, and their hoarding of wealth was constrained by their paternalist good faith.

Related to this presumed bond between private wealth and civic obligation in the late nineteenth century was a second assumption that held museum culture and historical conservation separate from the arena of conspicuous consumption. The founders and trustees of the American museum movement in the 1870s and 1880s considered it the function of the art museum to provide public instruction, to offer civic education for all the people by a presentation of the masterworks of the historical past. In the principal address dedicating the New York Metropolitan Museum in 1880, trustee Joseph C. Choate explained that the museum founders

> believed that the diffusion of a knowledge of art in its higher forms of beauty would tend directly to humanize, to educate and refine a practical and laborious people. . . . Art has become their best resource and most efficient educator, a vital and practical interest of the working millions.

Choate and his colleagues' conception of art was informed by a fundamental philosophical idealism, and by the notion of the inseparability of art and morality. Late nineteenth-century art theory was derived, as cultural historian Helen Horowitz has demonstrated, from Hegelianism, transcendentalism, and congregational religion. Horowitz identifies turn-of-the-century assumptions of "art's idealistic premises, that the role of art was to transcend material realities . . . to go beyond the useful to express the ideal." A recent study of the same period by Rémy Saisselin explains that American art theory and education were deeply influenced by the teachings of John Ruskin, who affirmed art's moral and religious functions. Ruskin's American followers, James Jackson Jarves and Charles Eliot Norton, were joined by religious leaders John Bascom and George Lansing Raymond in disseminating ideas concerning the role of art as an agent of collective moral uplift and social humanization.

The antimaterialistic conception of art shared by Metropolitan Museum founders was expressed not only in their assumption of the moral benefits of art for the masses but also in their appeals to potential wealthy patrons for donations. Choate offered this extraordinary passage in his dedication speech, which was meant to loosen the pockets of millionaire industrialists and financiers:

> Think of it, ye millionaires of many markets—what glory may yet be yours, if you . . . convert pork into porcelain, grain and produce into priceless pottery, the rude ores of commerce into sculptured marble, and railroad shares and mining stocks— things which perish without the using—into the glorified canvas of the world's masters, that shall adorn these walls for centuries. The rage is to hunt the philosopher's stone, to convert

all baser things into gold, which is but dross; but ours is the higher ambition to convert your useless gold into things of living beauty that shall be a joy to a whole people for a thousand years.

Choate's statement emphasized a long-term historical view that united a glorification of the masterpieces of the cultural past with a celebration of their preservation as a living patrimony for generations to come. Millionaires of the present were urged to "invest" in tradition, to serve as keepers of the cultural flame and as what the historian John Kouwenhoven has called "custodians of culture." This stewardship involved transcending the shifting, precarious, and instrumental world of the market and converting "base" or "useless" lucre into timeless, sacred objects of beauty for the temple of high culture.

The participants in the 1980s aristocratic movement do not share with their Gilded Age predecessors a commitment to the presumed unity between wealth and obligation, and no longer engage in social legitimation through civic education projects. The Gospel of Wealth under Ronald Reagan worships material success and self-centered individualism, and consigns the Social Gospel to the dustbin of "dependency." Further, the Reaganite aristocratic project unites the spheres of historical culture and conspicuous consumption kept separate by Gilded Age elites. Veblen's early twentieth-century giants of industrial capitalism have been replaced by the directors of advanced consumer capitalism, for whom conspicuous consumption has a very different meaning and function. Veblen's understanding of the phenomenon of conspicuous consumption hinged on a "leisure class" whose involvement in visible display was the mark of its remoteness from production. Atavistic and conservative, the leisure class announced its exemption from market activities by its cult of appearance. The dress and shoes of elite women in particular epitomized for Veblen the relationship between "industrial exemption and conspicuous consumption"; dress operated as the "insignia of leisure," the proclamation of freedom from utility and function. Rather than the mark of distance and exemption from the market, conspicuous consumption for the aristocratizing Reagan elite is the emphatic sign of involvement in it. Physical display, for Diana Vreeland, Bill Blass, Oscar de la Renta, Estée Lauder, and Ralph Lauren, is not the insignia of leisure but the essence of their work—selling images of self. The publicity for the lavish Yves Saint Laurent gala at the Metropolitan Museum, such as the huge color-photo spread in *W*, offered a showcase of celebrity evening wear destined to keep the wheels of the fashion market churning. The haute couture ensembles featured at the Met party were continually translated into licensed ready-to-wear versions, whose voluminous sales underwrite the expensive production of haute couture.

The transfer of conspicuous consumption from a leisure class to the corporate managers of appearance has transformed the art museum into another realm of consumer production. The activity of the 1980s group—as opposed to that of Veblen's conservative elite—is grounded in continuous change, in stimulating the insatiable novelty demanded by the consumer market. As the fashion designer joins other corporate managers in replacing Veblen's "captains of industry," the meaning and function of culture are irrevocably altered. Veblen's elite protected culture as a source of stability and tradition; Reagan's elite colonizes culture for consumerism. The Robber Barons of the Gilded Age were eager to serve as "custodians of culture"; they aimed to establish and preserve an artistic patrimony separate from the marketplace. The 1980s mass market moguls are cultural cannibals; they absorb the historical materials of art-museum exhibitions for the purposes of advertising, public relations, and sales campaigns. Rather than the domain in which to express the moral brake on conspicuous consumption, the museum becomes the extension of the department store and another display case for the big business of illusion making. The Metropolitan Museum's Saint Laurent exhibition and Polo / Ralph Lauren's "presentation" of "Man and the Horse" typify this shift from museum as cultural education to museum as commercial manipulation. Ralph Lauren's Polo ads appeal to "timeless" grace, "tradition," and history as a technique to sell clothes and life-style furnishings that recall those of the Edwardian gentry. Lauren considers the purpose of the Met "Man and the Horse" exhibition to be a mode of entry into the world that "inspired" his designs, the originating center of the "stylishness" he tries to evoke in Polo. If Joseph Choate proposed, in 1880, that millionaire industrialists convert "things which perish," convert "useless gold into things of living beauty that shall be a joy to a whole people for a thousand years," the museum sponsors assembled by Diana Vreeland in the 1980s aspire to convert things of living beauty into gold, into things which perish, into museum-processed commodities.

The annexing of museum culture for marketing and the repudiation of historical preservation also distinguish the 1980s aristocratizing elite from a more recent public figure, Jacqueline Kennedy. In her reign as First Lady, Mrs. Kennedy brought to the White House high style, couture fashion, and lavish entertainment that may appear similar to the opulence favored by the Nancy Reagan coterie. Yet Jacqueline Kennedy had a strong and vital commitment to history, and to connecting the past and present, through her work in monument restoration. Soon after her arrival at the White House, she embarked on a renovation of its interiors. "Years of mistreatment and neglect" had left the mansion filled with what she called "tasteless" combinations of miscellaneous bric-a-brac, which she likened to the furnishings of a second-class hotel. Mrs. Kennedy developed a plan to re-create the White House rooms using the original furnishings and decor exactly as they had been coordinated under President Monroe (1817–1825) "in the then-fashionable French Empire style." In addition, she scoured the basement of the mansion and the White House warehouse in Fort Washington, Maryland, for authentic objects from earlier presidencies: Rutherford B. Hayes's desk, Abraham Lincoln's china service, President Monroe's flatware. Assembling historical scholars of the applied arts to guide her, she set up the White House Fine Arts Committee to seek donations, not of money, but of "authentic furnishings reflecting the history and presidency of the United States." In this way furniture that had once belonged to Washington, Madison, and Lincoln reentered the White House quarters, and the state rooms have remained to this day exactly as Mrs. Kennedy restored them. She also established the White House Historical Association and the position of White House curator, to ensure the continuity of accurate preservation and historical presentation. In these ways Jackie Kennedy provided what her husband praised as a living historical legacy of the presidential past, destined to enrich the nation's understanding of its present and future.

The White House, which has become disfigured by incongruous additions and changes, has now been restored to what was planned by Washington. The White House is the property of the nation and, so far as it is compatible with living therein, it should be kept as it originally was for the same reasons we keep Mount Vernon as it originally was. . . . It is a good thing to preserve such buildings as historic monuments, which keep alive our sense of continuity with the nation's past.

Jackie Kennedy's "preoccupation with history" sets her apart from the 1980s aristocratizing elite with their powerful impulse to obliterate history. Mrs. Kennedy remained attached to an older tradition of aristocracy and obligation, of the moral exchange between the affluent and the less fortunate. The high-society followers of Mrs. Reagan and Mrs. Vreeland celebrate aristocracy as posture, as external trappings, and as luxury without responsibility. The dissolution of history at the center of this aristocratic consumerist elite, and its political meaning and function, can be traced to 1980 through a series of events featuring a common cast of characters and a shared set of themes. The year 1980 unfolds like a Chinese imperial triptych, beginning with Bloomingdale's, reappearing at Vreeland's Metropolitan Museum, and ending with Nancy Reagan's own project of redecorating the White House, which incorporated chinoiseries and repudiated the Kennedys' historicist legacy.

CHINA
AT BLOOMINGDALE'S
AND THE MET

1980–1981

Bloomingdale's China, 1980: "Baubles, Bangles,
and Bedazzling Things"

n September 1980 Bloomingdale's announced it had "unleashed the largest merchandising venture ever in the history of the store" by transporting the riches of China to New York. Advertisements declared that now consumers could travel to China without a passport. Embark on the journey to the East Side, urged the ads in the *New York Times*; in Bloomingdale's one can experience the "sights, sounds, smells and scents of China." The entire premises of the Lexington Avenue store were transformed into a vision of an opulent, hieratic China, land of emperors, mystery, and dazzling artisans feeding the emperors' relentless needs for magnificence. The outside of Bloomingdale's was bedecked with the banners representing the ancient Chinese martial arts: sabers and their exquisitely crafted blade cases. Inside the store's capacious halls, numerous veneered black and red screens were erected, turning the open space into a multiplicity of small, intimate compartments resembling a maze of shiny black boxes. Here the glistening "baubles, bangles, and be-dazzling things" of China, as they were called, were displayed. Among the varied objects bombarding the spectator-buyer with their shimmering surfaces were gold and jade bracelets, cinnabar bowls and plates, multicolored woven shawls, coral and garnet boxes, and short jackets and long robes shot through with gold threads, silks, and sequins.

The Chinese imports offered at the re-created Bloomingdale's were presented in the store's display information and in ads in three ways: as timeless, aristocratic, and rare. Each of the three characteristics reflected the peculiar selectivity with which Bloomingdale's marketers fashioned their image of the People's Republic. Bloomingdale's China was a prerevolutionary and preindustrial China, whose luxury artisans practiced the traditions, unbroken, of the emperors. It was a civilization construed as particularly gifted in the creation of delicate, artistic objects for intimate pleasures.

The metahistorical quality of Chinese civilization came through in the Bloomingdale's ads celebrating the "country steeped in forty centuries of opulence and ritual," whose "richness, mystery, and romance were barely touched since Marco Polo's journey seven hundred years ago." And in display cases, placards identified the "ancient craft of lacquer" and the "timeless weavers' art." The promotion literature also stressed that Bloomingdale's buyers, who spent months in China looking for merchandise, had performed an invaluable service for the Chinese people. The buyers' "tireless tracking," patient "sifting," and relentless efforts had led to the rediscovery of Chinese craft treasures, hidden from the public in the aftermath of the Cultural Revolution. From the "warehouses, back alleys, and small markets" in China, Bloomingdale's had rescued the essence of Chinese culture and was offering it as booty to gentrified New Yorkers.

Gone were the days when China was inseparable from Maoist uniforms, the monochrome caps and jackets beloved of the 1960s American counterculture. The uniformity of Mao's blues was replaced by the extravagant irregularity of ancient nobilities. The imperial tone was set by the sabers adorning the outer walls of the store. Inside, the store placards promised the "most spectacular dynasty of dazzlers this side of Peking." The dynastic dazzlers included woven rugs, "prerevolutionary pieces, each and every one"; coats and robes

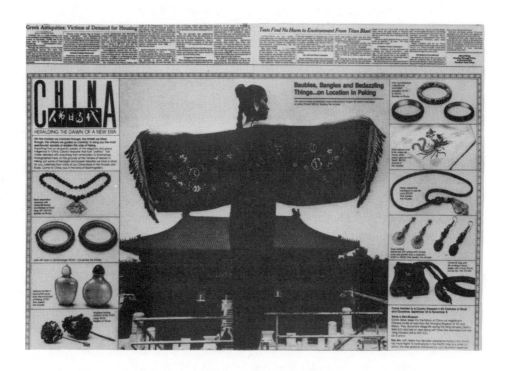

Bloomingdale's China ad, 1980

modeled on the magnificent handmade robes worn by the emperors; cloisonné jewelry that reproduced the styles of the Ch'ing dynasty; cinnabar tableware and boxes advertised as originally made for palace use; and objects like the "Double Happiness Ginger Jar," Bloomingdale's "reproduction of a T'ang dynasty treasure."

The packaging of China as timeless and aristocratic was complemented by the theme of its special devotion to the rare and handcrafted. The artifacts for sale at the Chinese Bloomingdale's were consistently presented as "precious and original." Display shelves in the store were filled with "hand-painted porcelain underglaze bowls," "hand-carved cinnabar coasters," and "handwoven rugs," whose "rare and original" qualities could be found "exclusively at Bloomingdale's." These craft objects and a multitude of others—"each one a work of art"—testified to what Bloomingdale's promoters called the special Chinese "concern for utmost quality and artistic merit."

Bloomingdale's glorification of China in the guise of a timeless, aristocratic civilization dedicated to the handicrafts revealed two fundamental contradictions. First, the dazzling artifacts from the People's Republic were not authentic vessels of ancient mysteries but rather the simulated products of a shrewd business alliance between the Bloomingdale's managers and the Communist Chinese government. Indeed, the Chinese imports were the first fruits of a new commercial agreement between the United States and China, which Bloomingdale's was among the first to cash in on. Eager to increase its exports abroad, China signed a 1979 trade agreement with the United States in which the Chinese offered to manufacture consumer and luxury items in China to the desired specifications of the American client.

A peculiar paradox enabled the Communist Chinese to cooperate with the center of consumer capitalism. In 1979 and 1980 China embarked on a new program, the "four modernizations," to help stimulate its much-needed economic development. The "four modernizations" included science, technology, industry, and technical education, which government officials stated would also provide the required components for a "new decade of socialist construction." As in other times in its history, China proposed to pave the roads of modern construction with the proceeds from the sale of its feudal heritage. Since the time of Marco Polo, China had struck a bargain with the West, ransoming off the rich, exotic artifacts of its imperial culture in exchange for the tools of modernization. In 1980 China was again eager to "export its cultural legacy," which had been prohibited under Mao as the domain of the "four olds" (language, art, customs, and clothes). The profits from the Bloomingdale's sales of simulated noble China would be used to pay the advisers from the Conoco, Fluor, and American Steel corporations that the Chinese had invited to help with its communist goal of the "four modernizations."

Bloomingdale's acted quickly on the new United States–China trade agreement and set to work establishing ties with Chinese craft manufacturers who would fill their orders. The items commissioned were designed by Bloomingdale's artists in New York, who projected their fantasies of the opulent, mysterious empire and ordered accordingly. This, then, was the origin of the "authentic" Chinese imports, envisioned in New York by Bloomingdale's designers and then custom-made, in China, with labels stating in both English and Chinese, "Made in China for Bloomingdale's." Thus Bloomingdale's image of China was fashioned on the basis of a double artifice: the objects that captured the "essence" of China were themselves first sketched out on Lexington Avenue, and then they were made in China exclusively for Bloomingdale's in manufactories set up especially for American export.

Bloomingdale's explicitly celebrated its own responsibility for creating China in its image. A *New Yorker* cartoon that showed Chinese factory managers stating that they had "to wait for Bloomingdale's instructions to begin production" was used by the store in its own ad campaign to illustrate its "newest expansion in China." Other ads credited Bloomingdale's own buyers for ensuring the standards and quality of Chinese products. One claimed that the beautiful handmade Chinese sweaters knit for Bloomingdale's were "developed one-on-one with the Chinese . . . to our standards, our American taste, with the Chinese attentiveness to quality and detail." Another rhapsodized, "Oh, the artisans we guided so carefully to bring you . . . everything that so eloquently speaks of the elegance and grace indigenous to China." And a third explained that the Bloomingdale's representatives on location in Beijing made sure that the Chinese objects "looked crafted, not made."

The second contradiction intrinsic to the presentation of China at Bloomingdale's emerged in relation to the "handmade" and "original" qualities attached to the merchandise. During the previous ten years Bloomingdale's had participated in a more general marketing movement, the arrival of the handcrafted item in the department store. In the nineteenth century, when the department store was born, it was perceived as the enemy of the handmade item. In Zola's *Au Bonheur des Dames* (1886), for example, the department store is presented as a ruthless, voracious monster, whose commitment to volume and fast turnover signaled the death of the small retail shop and the individual artisans who supplied it. In America, since the late 1970s, this assumption of a life-and-death struggle between the big department store and the individual artisan has been dramatically altered. Department stores have welcomed the craftsmen, reflecting and ex-

Bloomingdale's China wares

"Before we decide on our next expansion of the people's industry, shouldn't we check with Bloomingdale's?"

pressing Americans' attraction to the signed, individually rendered item. This absorption of the artisanal into the centers of consumer emporiums marks the ultimate reversal of the 1960s back-to-nature, back-to-the-homemade-crafts impulse. If the production of handmade use objects once expressed cultural rebellion, now department stores offer signed, individually crafted items, from chocolates to underwear, as the ultimate of purchasers' status symbols.

Bloomingdale's handicraft China was part of this broader change in merchandising over the past decade. The China show clarified a contradiction underlying the general trend of promoting "original" craft items in the department store. For although the Chinese plates, robes, coats, and jewelry at "Bloomie's" were surrounded by placards proclaiming their "rare," "original," and "handcrafted" character, the number and variety of items suggested their very lack of uniqueness.

How could scores of rugs and bins overflowing with cloisonné stick-pins be seen as "each and every one a work of art"? Although the items were at least partly handmade, they were hardly the fruits of a single, patient, and skilled artisan who worked as had those under imperial tutelage. The Bloomingdale's China wares had a claim on being handmade in that they were not made by machines. But the craft objects imported from China were produced at human assembly lines, where massive orders for hand-painted fans, bowls, plates, and clothes were filled by intense division of labor and specialization. The "timeless artisans" who supplied the Bloomingdale's shelves and racks worked at repetitive, painstaking tasks in which scores of skilled laborers contributed a monotonous small part in the creation of a single craft product.

If their production by sweated craft labor belied the handmade character of the Chinese items, their supposed "rare" and "unique" qualities were subverted by their very plethora. Bloomingdale's tried very hard to envelop the many objects on display in a distinction suggested by their history and lineage. Thus, as we have seen, scores of "Double Happiness Ginger Jars" were associated with the dynasty of their origin, and other items were labeled as reproductions of statues and relics of religious shrines. Yet the Bloomingdale's China spectator was assaulted by the sheer volume of the items and soon became anesthetized, as in all department stores, by the number and variety of the objects for sale. The stated sacred and imperial legacies of the objects dissolved in the kingdom of the commodity. The tags on the Chinese items leveled them into a single category, that of price. All the proclamations of distinction, of noble heritage, and of ritual use collapsed; underwear with "Made in China" labels, cinnabar coasters, miniature horse sculptures modeled on those of the emperors, and reprocessed imperial robes—all blurred into one mesmerizing imperative: How much does it cost?

China at the Metropolitan Museum, 1980: Diana Vreeland and Chinese "Opium"

No sooner had the Bloomingdale's China project begun to wind down than a new celebration of China as the crucible of luxury, aristocracy, and rare artistic crafts was born. In December 1980 the Metropolitan Museum of Art opened an exhibition at its Costume Institute, "The Manchu Dragon: Costumes of China, the Ch'ing Dynasty, 1644–1912." Organized and installed by Diana Vreeland and her assistants, the Met show displayed magnificent Chinese imperial robes. The robes were not suspended in cases as in other costume exhibits; they were draped on mannequins' bodies and set in rooms reproducing the palace and temple settings in which the robes were originally worn. In this way Vreeland aspired to transport the viewer into the authentic atmosphere of Chinese imperial culture. Protected for centuries in China behind the walls of the emperors' quarters, the "Forbidden City," the opulence, refinement, and delicacy of what Vreeland called "the land of jade" were now exposed to public view.

The Met's China dragon court robe

Significantly, in the months before the Met show opened, many of the same precious Chinese robes to be exhibited at the Met had been on display at Bloomingdale's, where a special museum had been established for the duration of the China sales campaign. The Metropolitan exhibition was on the surface very different from the Bloomingdale's project. At the department store the real Chinese robes had been difficult to distinguish from the panoply of reproductions offered for sale in close proximity; the Met show focused only on the rare, authentic robes, lifting them out of the marketplace into the citadel of scholarship, connoisseurship, and historical explication. Yet despite the presumed difference between the consumerist and high cultural versions of China, the 1980 Met museum show shared the themes and selectivity of the Bloomingdale's packaging of China. The theme of the Met exhibition was the celebration of China as a timeless, aristocratic culture devoted to artistic crafts. And the ethos of the Metropolitan's curator, Diana Vreeland, was closer to a marketing strategy than to the task of historical education. The Metropolitan's Chinese robes show emerged as a perfect pendant to the Bloomingdale's presentation of China preceding it; it projected fantasies of wealth, power, and leisure attached to an ancient imperial civilization and displayed them in the form of a fashion show.

The Met exhibition extended Bloomingdale's vision of China as a timeless world "steeped in forty centuries of ritual and opulence." The costume show covered the entire span of the Manchu reign, a period of almost three hundred years. Historical specificity was entirely lacking from the exhibition displays; the only guiding principle was the emphasis on the long reign of luxury and opulence signified by the rulers' magnificent clothes and elegant furniture. The exhibit lacked basic information to enable the viewer to differentiate the various rulers and their historical contexts. The tags on the artifacts identified the robes, the materials out of which they were made, and their historical provenance, usually generalized as the "Ch'ing dynasty," which thus placed them somewhere between the seventeenth and twentieth centuries.

The aristocratic and artisanal character of the Bloomingdale's China show also reappeared as the organizing themes at the Met. The exquisitely crafted stuffs of the emperors filled the Met halls with the original "dynastic dazzlers" celebrated in simulated form at Bloomie's. Lacquer screens, carved jade jewelry, celadon porcelains, pen quills and inkstands studded with precious stones, ivory and cinnabar miniature sculptures carved into women's hair combs—these were some of the objects crafted to the standards of the rulers. In the center of one of the exhibition halls, Vreeland re-created a royal boudoir, framed by a carved-wood pagoda top and bright red silk linens across the bed. The emperors' presence was felt throughout in the shimmering surfaces of their multicolored robes, and in the costumes worn by their wives and concubines. In one tiny corner near the imperial boudoir appeared a glimpse of the China beyond the ruler. A "Chinese coolie" was displayed, standing on a stepped platform, dressed entirely in a simple white shroud and hat. The white simplicity of the designated coolie contrasted sharply with the breathtaking colors of the imperial clothes and interiors by which it was quickly overwhelmed.

Like the contradictions in the Bloomingdale's project, the Met's presentation of China as timeless, aristocratic, and artisanal was subverted by the visibility of very timely elements in the exhibition. The attempt to reconstitute Chinese court life and clothes was mired in a thick layer of Western fantasy, specifically the fantasy of the fashion show designer and promoter. The influence of Diana Vreeland brought about the suspension of the normal categories of scholarly accuracy, historical erudition, and artistic connoisseurship with which museum shows are normally mounted. Vreeland approached the Chinese robes with the declaration, "I'm looking for the most far-fetched perfection . . . and I'm terrible on facts. But I always have an idea. If you have an idea, you're well ahead!" The artifacts of Chinese civilization were subjected to the antihistorical drama of a woman who had invented the "composite photo" for maximum shock effect.

The quintessentially Vreelandian perspective imposed on Chinese civilization emerged at the Met show in two ways. The first was in the use of mannequins. Immediately on entering the gallery, the spectator was thrown into a bizarre underworld closer to the more extreme pages of *Vogue* than to Chinese imperial courts. In a dimly lit room, one heard high-pitched ancient Chinese music, and one's senses were assaulted by a very powerful smell. Vreeland had drenched

Summer robe of state for a high-ranking official

the room in a fragrance that she explained as capturing the essence of China—her friend Yves Saint Laurent's new perfume, called Opium. Opium may have been the essence of China to Vreeland, but, as Orville Schell reminds us, the drug had been originally imported into China by Western merchants in the eighteenth and nineteenth centuries, where, in contravention of Chinese law, they had traded the drug "at enormous profit for silk, tea, and silver." Opium, Schell continues, had been the traditional source of conflict between China and the West, for it epitomized the unequal and humiliating character of foreign treaties and actions. The 1980 Saint Laurent Opium fragrance drenching the Ch'ing dynasty Chinese emperors' robes re-created the historical license of Western mis-appropriation of China and added a startling new irony to the record of Western representations of the East. The sights of China immediately greeted the viewer who had just recovered from the sounds and smells. In a long row stood, in varying languorous poses, ten female mannequins bedecked in court robes and ceremonial costumes. The mannequins had elongated features, especially marked in their faces, hands, ears, and feet. Tall and ungainly, the "Chinese" mannequins in costume had faces painted in different color schemes—brown, pink, yellow, red, and black. Their pointy faces and ears gave them the strange look of Mister Spock in "Star Trek." Whatever their origin, the mannequins embodied an extension of the pages of an elite fashion magazine rather than representative types who might have worn Chinese courtly vestments.

The triumph of fashion illusionism over Chinese history appeared in a second way. The labeling of the objects in the show focused exclusively on their exquisite surfaces. Not only was explanation of historical provenance missing, but the exhibit labels offered no sense of the meaning and function of the Chinese robes and decorative arts within their national context. The labels delineated, in great detail, the richness and variety of the materials that went into the creation of the robes and other court costumes. This strategy resembled the descriptions used at fashion shows, where the dress paraded is complemented by the stated explanation of its contents. At the Met's China show the spectator was endlessly bombarded with tags stating "embroidered wool tabby, highlighted with gold silk threads and brocaded velvet"; "informal suit, silk damask topped with sequined scarf," and so forth. In all the labels, the anachronistic jargon of fashion talk like "informal suits," "at-home wear," and "summer dress" was matched by the obsessive attentiveness to the expensive materials quite clearly visible on the surface of the imperial garments.

At the time of the Chinese robes exhibition, reviewers like Rita Reif commented that "there was more fantasy than fact in these displays." Reif went on to note one glaring inaccuracy in the show, which altered the meaning and function of the imperial robes: they were not worn for public display, but for private worship. Reif remarked that the magnificent robes were always worn underneath a long, plain black overcoat; only the borders of the brightly colored robes were ever visible on the emperor. In addition, Reif indicated that Vreeland had mixed and matched Chinese raiment indiscriminately. Never would a Chinese wife or courtesan of the emperor have worn an "outfit" like the ones created by Vreeland. Reif claimed that the mannequins displayed the "layered look" of 1970s fashion designers rather than the style of any Chinese historical period.

There was another visible distortion in the Met's China show, which sapped the Chinese robes of their primary significance and function. The essence of the Chinese robe was not on its surface, but in the deep symbolic meaning that it expressed. The Chinese robes operated in a cosmological system where all material objects were redolent with meaning. Not only wool tabby and gold thread adorned the emperor's robes, but symbols of his authority and of his place in a sacred hierarchy binding the gods and their earthly representatives. The imperial robes had as their insignia the five-fingered dragon, a symbol exclusively reserved for the ruler. The emperor's robe was a microcosm of the heavenly macrocosm; all types of natural forces were splayed across the robe—fire and water, sky and air—summarizing all of creation on the body of the emperor. Encased in the robe, the ruler's body symbolized the axis and his head the apex of the universe. Rigid codes governed the symbolism of all garments, and each person in the Chinese social system, from bureaucrat and palace guard to scholar and soldier, had a particular outer sign to mark his rank. Thus, the clothes at the Met show all originally expressed the membership of their bearer in a caste system, and the signs and designs on the outer garb were emblems of position in the hierarchy of man and nature. In Diana Vreeland's hands, the links between surface, symbol, meaning, and social function so central to the Chinese imperial garments were eliminated. The "Empress of Clothes" pressed the Chinese artifacts into the service of a new fad for gilded and glossy outfits befitting a new American cult of visible wealth and power.

The devotees of Diana Vreeland and the contemporary cult of opulence surfaced at a grand celebration housed at the Met two weeks before the opening of the Chinese robes exhibition. On the evening of December 8, 1980, the Council of Fashion Designers sponsored a lavish gala to greet the show and pay tribute to its artificer, Vreeland. The *New York Times* characterized the christening party as "Fashion's Big Night at the Met." Seven hundred people paid three hundred dollars apiece to dine on the obligatory coquilles Saint-Jacques and

A court robe for an empress

fillet of beef, to watch Chinese fireworks, and to get an exclusive preview of the show.

The designers sponsoring the Chinese evening at the Met were longtime associates of Diana Vreeland, among them Yves Saint Laurent, Bill Blass, Oscar de la Renta, Adolfo, and Halston. Led by Blass, they created a party theme à la chinoise to capture the "proper air of mystery" intrinsic to China. The Met's Great Hall and dining area were transformed into a "Red Palace." Red carpets graced all the floors of the party chambers, which were lit from above by red spotlights. The grand reflecting pool around which the dinner guests sat was surrounded by huge banners hung from the ceiling. The tables were laid with black tablecloths and red napkins, and enlivened by red glazed vases filled with yellow lilies and sprays of quince. The ironic overtones of such a "red China" seemed to bother no one; the fashion council created its version to echo the luxury and exoticism captured in the exhibition's dazzling displays.

According to all reports, the splendor of China soon paled when compared to the lavish opulence exhibited by the party's American participants. "Fashion's big night at the Met" used China as a backdrop; the real show was in the array of new clothes designed by the party's sponsors and paraded on the partygoers. A new line of costumes was launched at the Met—"luxurious dresses" that "overshadowed the grandeur of the imperial robes." Stately Nancy Kissinger arrived in an original by Adolfo, the exclusive designer who was busy preparing Nancy Reagan's first inaugural suit. Diana Vreeland wore a shimmering gold jacket set off by a black skirt. Two representatives from Bonwit Teller's in "glittering dresses" promoted the sumptuous look of the new season's fashions. A Bloomingdale's executive arrived at the party in a multicolored, embroidered Chinese robe.

The Met party and its glorification of aristocratic Chinese culture coincided with President-Elect and Mrs. Reagan's December 1980 trip to New York, where they were joined at private dinners by fashion moguls Bill Blass and Oscar de la Renta. Nancy Reagan collected Chinese porcelains and lacquer tables, and revealed that her initial project as First Lady would be the redecoration of the White House private quarters to accommodate her exquisite Chinese decorative pieces. Two weeks after the Met party, the *New York Times* devoted its cover story to Françoise and Oscar de la Renta. Splashed across the Sunday magazine was a huge color photo of the rich and elegant designer couple, she in a blazing gold tunic and a collar six strands thick with pearls; he in a sleek black suit. The article, by Francesca Stanfill, was titled "Living Well Is Still the Best Revenge." Stanfill celebrated the "rarefied taste" and powerful wealth of the

Nancy Kissinger for Adolfo, on the cover of W
(Thomas Iannaccone/W)

couple, "distinguished," she stated, by their "sense of luxury" and the fact that "they have no fear of ostentation, nor are they inhibited by the pressure of discretion that often characterizes those with old fortunes." The fortune of Dominican-born Oscar de la Renta (né Renta) had been made in the mid-1970s, "not by shrewd marketing or even avant-garde designing, but by an unerring taste, and, to a great extent, a familiarity with his affluent clientele." De la Renta's speciality was extravagance, which usually took the form of massive ruffles attached to flamboyant skirts and evening gowns. While these luxury fashions had been the preserve of a small coterie of the wealthy for a decade, a new clientele and public presence now focused on the de la Rentas.

Stanfill associated the de la Rentas with a shift in American high society, a shift she predicted would be expressed in the Reagan White House. She identified the de la Rentas as part of a "new professional elite": "the very rich, the very powerful," the representatives of "current talent and current fame." This elite, according to Stanfill, was different from previous ones. This was no "leisure jet set," nor a society filled with bearers of old money and old family names. The de la Rentas were at the center of a "phalanx" of the "working upper-crust," a nouveau riche group that represented the fusion of society with big business. Fashion designers were a central part of this new elite, as managers of international licensing empires and as media celebrities binding their products to their personal identities. This was a group marked by "the energy, incentive, fearlessness, and aggressiveness of the ambitious." Vreeland was identified in the article as another figure in this new elite: "Now everything is power and money and how to use them both," Vreeland declared.

Stanfill went on to describe how the de la Rentas cloaked their ambition in elegant, opulent surroundings in a series of country and city residences whose overstuffed, cozy interiors were filled with refined luxury items. Françoise de la Renta, renowned for her talents as a decorator, arranged her rooms as "sybaritic backdrops" for her weekly salons; "masses of Rothschild lilies, flocked red velvet walls edged in *faux marbre*, silk upholstered Second Empire chairs, mother-of-pearl cabinets, windows swagged in heavy, fringed silk": these were some of the vessels of the de la Rentas' ineffable taste. Françoise told the *Times* reporter that she had developed her style as a decorator by studying great works of French literature, especially Balzac. "One thing that is very noticeable in Balzac is the *demimondaine*." She smiled. "One can learn a hell of a lot from the *demimondaine*."

The use of the motto "Living well is the best revenge" in relation to the unchecked pursuit of wealth, as symbolized by the de la Rentas, had undergone a telling transformation. A Spanish proverb, the phrase originated as a statement of philosophical resignation to fate: God was cruel, the world was difficult and painful, and one had to bear it with the understanding of an individual's limited power to control it. The motto was popularized in America through its association with the F. Scott Fitzgerald circle in the 1920s. Gerald Murphy, an American expatriate in France who socialized with the Fitzgeralds and Ernest Hemingway, invoked the saying in the context of the bohemianism, nonconformity, and bitterness that followed the devastation of World War I. Murphy and his coterie proposed a life of license in isolation as a reaction to the shattering of all ideals by the war. In 1980–1981, "living well is the best revenge" had gone from being associated with the anguished withdrawal of postwar hedonists to being tied to the raucous centrality of elite Reagan supporters. Rather than having to do with wreaking revenge on a world that had exposed moral ideals as illusions, the slogan now implied revenge on the poor, who were considered undeserving.

The Reagan Inauguration: Opulence and Chinoiseries

The inauguration of Ronald Reagan in January 1981 channeled the celebration of luxury, and its presumed historical carriers, from the salons of the New York fashion designers to the chambers of state. The image-makers of aristocratic privilege in clothes and interior design were not only associates of curator Diana Vreeland but friends of Nancy and Ron. And the cult of visible wealth expressed in culture and merchandising was transposed into the policies of social repudiation pursued by the Reagan White House.

The Reagan presidential inaugural festivities trumpeted the arrival of opulence at the highest levels of state. Commentators like R. Williams, Laurence Leamer, and Michael Kinsley noted the "staggering splendor" and coronation tone to the affair. President Reagan requested that invitees don the formal morning "stroller" suit, popular at the time of the Prince of Wales, for the swearing-in ceremony. Nancy Reagan's gowns, gloves, embroidered handbags, hand-sewn shoes, and floor-length minks changed constantly before the eyes of the public. Outfitting Nancy were her longtime friends, designers Bill Blass, Adolfo, and Galanos, who garbed the First Lady in their new concept of the "sybaritic outfit." At one of the gala inaugural events the Reagans and the Bushes were treated to an evening of Hollywood entertainment, taped live for television. Frank Sinatra organized the evening, and the performers' stage was set directly opposite a platform on which four plush winged chairs were arranged. Nancy and Ron looked like the king and queen observing their many jesters; Mrs. Bush sat shimmering in an embroidered Chinese robe.

The Reagan inauguration set the tone for a full-fledged cult of visible luxury and unrestrained flaunting of wealth. The $16 million inaugural extravaganza witnessed the arrival of the millionaire Californians and Hollywood stars in Washington, where they inched their way through a crush of limousines and gorged on endless delicacies. A startling contrast to the rich Reagan revelers was seen in one telling incident, when the Washington city derelicts and bag ladies made their way into Union Station, crashing the party reserved for those who had bought the one-thousand-dollar entry tickets. The hungry poor, whom Reagan aides were soon to dub wily cheaters, helped themselves to the "lobster bisque, shrimp merlin, escargots, and vitello alla geatano" heaped on forty tables. The mingling of the super rich and the street people under the iron-and-glass sheds of Union Station offered a startling juxtaposition of the two worlds.

The dedication of Nancy Reagan to display brought new attention to the elite fashion designers; the *Times* noted in January that "their business is booming, despite the recession." Nancy's cult of snobbism in appearance also legitimized lavish ornamental femininity. Nancy had been, for over twenty years, a "professional lady" who spent her days with Betsy Bloomingdale, Jean Smith, Mary Jane Wick, and Marion Jorgenson on the complex work of maintaining a youthful and elegant appearance. The *New York Times* and other papers indicated that a new kind of woman had arrived in the train of Nancy Reagan and her sumptuous adornments. This was not an eastern

The Reagans en route to inaugural balls, January 21, 1981
(AP/Wide World Photos)

woman but a Sunbelt beauty, who "cared about style and did not want to look unobtrusive." She was "upwardly mobile, suburban, with a sensibility founded on buying power and an unabashed appreciation of luxury." Nancy represented this woman's values; she unleashed a new era of style, a style that melded the nouveau-riche values of the de la Rentas and Blasses with the rugged individualism of western entrepreneurs and their wives. "We've worked for this," the wife of a Texas real estate developer at the inaugural ball was quoted as saying. "We're proud and we're not afraid to show it." The sense that hard work should be rewarded was the theme expressed by other women attending the ball. Bedecked in ruffled satin gowns by Blass, de la Renta, and Galanos, and gleaming in egg-shaped rubies, diamonds, ostrich feathers, and ermine capes, these women noted how they were "tired of having to apologize for ourselves." Nancy Reagan provided these women with a "lift": "Now we know it's all right to buy grand clothes again without looking out of place." The *Times* article concluded that in some ways these women were the Cinderella wives of Horatio Alger husbands, who offered visible proof to everyone beneath them on the social scale that "they can do it too."

Vreeland's Allure and Reagan's Political Culture, 1980

The "new woman" at the inaugural balls expressed in fashion the ethos of Reagan's politics of rugged, venturesome individualism and its ideology of deserved rewards. From the beginning of his administration, Reagan was relentless in his declarations of the need for a return to the old American values of individual effort and risk-taking, and the upward mobility to follow from both. Reagan justified the inaugural luxury as evidence of the riches that were obtainable in American society through hard work and talent.

Many writers have pointed out the anachronisms and ironies of Reagan's free-enterprise ideology; the rough-and-tough individualist idealized by the rancher-president has little basis in either the marketplace of advanced corporate capitalism or the personal success story of the president himself. The president never liked to work, and he prospered less from individual effort than from a combination of luck, corporate power, and the uncanny ability to please. He got his start

Betsy Bloomingdale in inaugural Washington
(Lucian Perkins/The Washington Post)

in both economic and political life as the "corporate ambassador" for General Electric in the 1950s. He was drafted into gubernatorial politics by millionaire California conservatives Tuttle, Salvatori, and Rubel in 1964. And few members of Reagan's inner circle of friends and advisers—Alfred Bloomingdale, Justin Dart, William French Smith, or Charles Wick—owed their wealth and position to the operations of isolated individuals striving in the free market. Reagan's appeal to ordinary Americans to aspire to freedom, self-reliance, moral rectitude, and individual diligence is a masterful exercise of the "politics of symbolism."

The Reagan politics of theater and of elitist individualism received a striking cultural expression in the work and writings of Diana Vreeland. A few months before the opening of the Met China show Vreeland published a book called *Allure*. The text of *Allure* revealed that Vreeland nourished fantasies not only of opulent nobilities of the past but of cruelty and decadence in the present.

Allure was a mixture of memoirs and oracles from the queen of the elite fashion world, whose taste and sense of style had been nurtured in over thirty years of editing *Vogue* and *Harper's Bazaar*. A large folio volume with huge black-and-white fashion photos interspersed with textual comments by Vreeland, the book collected Vreeland's favorite fashion photographers, from the Baron de Meyer to Irving Penn, and her favorite beautiful women, among them the Vicomtesse de Ribes, Greta Garbo, Evita Perón, Gertrude Stein, Marilyn Monroe, and the Duchess of Windsor. The dust jacket characterized as "by turns witty, sharp, extravagant, and cruel" the "Vreelandian perspective" which took the reader through a "luxurious, gossip-ridden world that DV knows so well."

One clear theme of *Allure* was aristocratic revival and its contemporary aesthetic emulation. Vreeland glorified the "stature," "inner exaltation," "bones," and "strength" of the Duchesse de Gramont, the beauty of Russian noblewoman Princess Yousoupoff, and the visible royalty of Princess Bebar, wife of the last sultan of the Ottoman Empire. Born in France and brought up in England, Mrs. Vreeland (née Diana Hoffman Dalziel) recalled that the coronation of George V in 1911 was a central event in her early life. She loved the "correctness and perfect design" of the horses, carriages, and military men in procession and lamented that such grace "survives today only in the army, the navy, the church, and in royalty." In other places in the book Vreeland hinted at the many members of the upper crust that she knew personally. Invoking no less an authority than Marcel Proust, one of her favorite authors, she passed scathing comments on other people's social backgrounds: she described Maria Callas as "common as mud"; Josephine Baker, the music hall performer, as "a total Parisienne, even though she was a laundress's daughter from St. Louis"; and, in the inverse, Vreeland remarked of Elsa Maxwell that "she looked vulgar; her nose was vulgar. She looks like a cook on her day off . . . of course, she no doubt had just been dining with a king—always kings!! She had the best taste in people."

Much of Vreeland's book aspired to define the meaning of true "elegance" and "allure." Vreeland acknowledged that aristocracies of the blood were gone; female aristocracies of the spirit could be cultivated through style and taste, manifested in the ineffable qualities of "elegance" and "allure." The meaning of "allure" was ambiguous in Vreeland's account. Allure is "something that *holds* you; it is something around you like a perfume or a scent. It's like memory—it pervades." In another section Vreeland distinguished fashion from elegance. Fashion is transient; "elegance is innate." It is a quality, according to Vreeland, possessed by certain animals, like gazelles, and women like Audrey Hepburn. The clearest definition Vreeland arrived at was "Elegance is refusal."

Vreeland's "witty, sharp, extravagant" tone, and her snobbish celebration of old and new aristocracies, had long been her trademarks. In the 1930s, when Mrs. Vreeland began writing for *Harper's Bazaar*, she established a column, "Why Don't You . . . ?" which amused Depression readers with bits of advice like "Why don't you convert your ermine coat into a bathrobe?" and "Why don't you wash your hair with champagne?" For Vreeland then, as now, all of this was grand posturing and playacting. When and whether she ever had real contact with European royalty and nobility is unclear. According to Jesse Kornbluth, Vreeland never had any formal education to speak of, trained briefly with the Ziegfeld Follies chorus girls as a dancer, and then ran a lingerie shop in London that specialized in black underwear. By her own admission, her world was a stage: "Performance is all I cared about as a child and it's all I care about now." Kornbluth characterized Vreeland as a shrewd individualist and ambitious businesswoman who had to work hard to subsidize her aristocratic affectations: "Though fated to be remembered as a high-society fashion oracle, Diana Vreeland has, all these years, been one of our greatest actresses, systematically parading her precariously luxurious life as a way of earning her daily *madeleine.*"

Less amusing and more pernicious themes surfaced in *Allure,* articulated in scathing and sadistic tones, suggesting the underside of the aristocratic revival. Vreeland had a long history of insidious statements, from the time in her 1930s columns that she recommended "Why don't you wear bare knees and long white knitted socks as Unity Mitford does when she takes tea with Hitler at the Carlton in Munich?" In 1980 Diana Vreeland sprinkled *Allure* with her memoirs of the 1930s. At one point she discussed the German spas and chuckled about her German doctor's prediction of mass murder:

> At the Kurhaus, in Freiburg-im-Breisgau, Reed and I would take baths and massages in the Black Forest. Every morning Dr. Govens would apply the Grenz ray to my sinuses. In the coming war they were going to release it and everyone in sight would be dead—they'd tell you all this. "Ooo," I'd say, "I can hardly wait; you Germans are so busy—such busy-bodies!"

Sadism and violence appeared in *Allure,* in the service of Vreeland's commitment to shock. She recounted how she discovered the composite photo for *Vogue* as a capstone to her career objective of not being boring or predictable. "I think laying out a beautiful picture in a beautiful way is a bloody bore. . . . The most boring thing on earth is to be of the world of what you do. That means people only expect from you what they think they'll get. That to me isn't the Big Time." Vreeland claimed that "you've got to blow the picture right across the page and down the side, crop it, cut it in half, do something with it!" Her violent artificing led her to "put arms and legs and everything else together" in a single layout, the composite photo. Faces were always missing from these spreads, which made *Vogue* notorious in the 1960s. Cutting up and mixing body parts of different models on a page, Vreeland declared, "I want arms! I want legs! I want hands!" Another of her innovations for *Vogue* was painting a white model shiny black with shoe polish and studding her eyes, breasts, and arms

Diana Vreeland and Lord Snowden (© Sonia Moskowitz 1986)

with diamonds, as testimony to the fact that "there's no place in the world where there's a vein of precious stone that doesn't belong to people of color. And they look so marvelous in jewels. . . . But a true black hand, however black, would have been . . . banal."

Allure depicted the shoe-polish-sprayed model and the dismembered elements of composite fashion photos. It also included a huge five-page insert that Vreeland had commissioned, though it was even too barbaric for *Vogue*. Vreeland thought it would be amusing, and shocking, to photograph an eye-lift operation. *Allure* published this photo spread, which *Vogue* had censored, illustrating with magnified camera lenses all phases of the cutting, lifting, and grafting of the eye skin. Vreeland said these pictures captured the fact that "I adore artifice!"

Diana Vreeland cultivated detachment and disengagement; the meaning and substance of her statements and her photos were always subordinated to the creation of effect, as long as it was not a bore. An omnipotence fantasy ruled these illusions; they were filled with the sense that the world could be shaped and reshaped in the cutting hands and bizarre eyes of its Vreelandian maker.

Vreeland's main message in *Allure*, that "elegance is refusal," had not only sexual but social implications. "We mustn't be afraid of snobbism and absurdity. And we musn't be afraid of luxury—there are no pictures of poverty here!" she exclaimed. *Allure* was a big seller in 1980, and has been since. In 1982 it received the Annual Rodeo Drive Gala Award in Los Angeles. Along the Beverly Hills street, the home of the exclusive boutiques where Nancy Reagan had shopped for her first inaugural wardrobe, Vreeland's book was displayed in every window, with costly jewels, scarves, shoes, and clothes wrapped around it. DV did talk once about poverty in *Allure*, explaining that when Elsa Maxwell lost all her money, she took it in style— when her piano and furniture were repossessed, she "performed an entire opera" for Vreeland, "slapping it out on those big, fat thighs of hers." Perhaps this was the fantasy of poverty that the Rodeo Drive merchants wished to nurture.

TWO

FABRICATION AND FRANCOPHILIA

THE FÊTES DE FRANCE
AT THE MET AND
BLOOMINGDALE'S
1981–1984

etween 1981 and 1984 the aristocratic tendency in culture and consumption gained momentum. Now the national ground of noble emulation shifted from China to France, extending the ironic transfiguration of a historical center of social revolution into an ahistorical treasure trove of irrepressible aristocratic grace. Between 1981 and 1983 Vreeland staged three French shows: "The Eighteenth-Century Woman," whose prototype was a lavishly decorated French noblewoman; "La Belle Epoque," a tribute to the stylish descendant of the eighteenth-century woman in pre–World War I France; and "Twenty-Five Years of Yves Saint Laurent," a celebration of the continuity of aristocratic haute couture in the modern period.

The passage from imperial China to Old Regime and Belle Epoque France had striking historical parallels; it echoed the pattern of aristocratic revivals in other historical periods. In the eighteenth century French aristocratic elites were swept by a wave of fondness for "chinoiseries," a consumer fad for the noble crafts of China. Oriental motifs and scenes were incorporated into French rococo interior design, landscape gardening, dress patterns, and porcelains. The artist François Boucher executed a print series called *Paysages Chinoises*, illustrating imaginary scenes of Chinese life, landscapes, and customs. Boucher's prints were pure Western fantasy, projecting Chinese figures with Western features wandering through improbable landscapes. French aristocrats in the mid-eighteenth century pressed the delicate Chinese arts into the service of political insulation and withdrawal: in the decades preceding the French Revolution, "chinoiseries" offered exotic fantasies and private escape from politics and social crisis. A new type of private room, the *singerie*, appeared in mid-eighteenth-century France, a small hand-decorated chamber for intimate indulgence. Here French nobles could enjoy the delights of painted walls depicting monkeys, Frenchwomen, and Chinese coolies romping through the grasses of a fantastic *fête champêtre*.

The progression of the Vreeland shows from imperial China to eighteenth-century France to the Belle Epoque revealed a second stage of historical parallels. If eighteenth-century French aristocrats themselves had revived imperial Chinese crafts, Belle Epoque French elites had a love affair with the eighteenth century. The Belle Epoque was marked by a full-fledged revival of eighteenth-century French aristocratic crafts, and the chinoiseries incorporated in them. The characters recovered in Vreeland's Belle Epoque show, such as Marcel Proust, the Count Robert de Montesquiou-Fézensac, and the Countess Greffulhe, were all avid collectors of the French rococo arts, which they worshipped nostalgically as the artifacts of a culture of grace and hierarchy destroyed by revolution and mass culture in the nineteenth century.

While there was a neat fit between the revival of China in eighteenth-century France and the revival of the eighteenth century in Belle Epoque France and the similar progression of the Vreeland shows, the meaning of the aristocratic revival in 1980s America was quite different from the previous French fads of noble emulation. For in the eighteenth century and in the Belle Epoque, the French revivals were pursued as a form of withdrawal and insulation from politics. Chinoiserie for the eighteenth-century French elites and rococo revival for 1890s French aristocratic aesthetes were forms of private protest

Eighteenth-century chinoiserie: porcelain potpourris

Boucher's chinoiseries

against a hostile and eruptive society; the escape into exotic fantasy and feminine grace provided a delicate buffer from an ungovernable external world. The aristocratic invocation in the 1980s had the inverse meaning from these historical precedents: rather than a form of intimate, impotent insulation from politics, the American movement was the arena for the assumption of power by the new elite. Nancy Reagan's renovation of the White House bedroom, which included hand-painted Chinese wallpaper and a huge, bristling French rococo mirror, was featured for public viewing in the *Architectural Digest* of December 1981. And the parties that inaugurated each Vreeland show offered public visibility and powerful affirmation to the elite flocking to aristocratic revival in 1980s America. These French shows were the occasions for their full-fledged wresting of both the political and cultural reins—an act of unabashed confidence rather than the resentful isolation that marked revivals past. The Reagan political and economic program had made this symbolic group coronation possible.

At their terminus in Saint Laurent luxury and clientele, the Met

historical French shows assumed a twofold character as self-fulfilling prophecy. First, Vreeland's peculiar historical re-creations of the eighteenth-century woman and La Belle Epoque prepared the way for the arrival of the opulent elite of the 1980s. At the same time, the shows offered this elite a comforting and titillating portrait of their adopted historical predecessors. What Vreeland called the "dancing, dreaming, and splendid" women of eighteenth-century France and the "naughty decadents" of the 1890s were each presented as unconstrained in their extravagant actions, as untainted by worldly engagements, as unchallenged in their power and indulgence.

Vreeland's "The Eighteenth-Century Woman": Feminism, Hedonism, and the Old Regime Aristocracy

On December 12, 1981, the public was initiated into Diana Vreeland's newest museum creation, an exhibition devoted to the "Eighteenth-

Century Woman." Chinese imperial robes doused in Saint Laurent's Opium were replaced by expansive hoop dresses of aristocratic women in late Old Regime France. This time Vreeland sprayed the galleries surrounding the costumes with the Guerlain fragrance Nahema. The cost of restoring and installing the dresses, along with the expense of assembling "authentic" eighteenth-century accessories and interior decor, was subsidized by a grant from Merle Norman cosmetics.

The time period covered by the "Eighteenth-Century Woman" exhibit ostensibly ranged from 1690 to 1790, but the main focus of the show was the period from 1720 to 1789. The 130 costumes included a few representatives from Denmark, England, Italy, the Netherlands, and Sweden, but the majority of the outfits were French. Following her practice with the Chinese imperial robes, Vreeland aspired to situate the eighteenth-century costumes within their specific environments. The dresses were thus displayed amidst a wide range of eighteenth-century accoutrements—painted fans, laces, hats, jewelry, gloves, slippers, furniture, porcelains, fashion manuals, and prints. The placement of the eighteenth-century woman within a re-created interior was particularly appropriate, for in the mid-eighteenth century, interior space was defined as distinctively feminine. The woman, draped in delicate layers of silk, taffeta, and lace, was considered an integral part of the ensemble of interior decor; her shape and clothing harmonized with the fragile, diminutive furnishings and objets d'art of the private interior. In this period in France, the highest compliment paid to a woman was that she resembled Sèvres porcelain, and Sèvres porcelain, in turn, was described by anthropomorphically female names such as "trembleuses," "rose du Barry," and the like.

Despite the generic title "The Eighteenth-Century Woman," the woman Vreeland celebrated as representative of her era and her gender was the eighteenth-century aristocratic woman. Her prototypes were Mme. du Barry, Mme. de Pompadour, Marie Leczinska, and Marie Antoinette—mistresses or wives of the French kings. These women were singled out in the Vreeland show for their wit, style, elegance, aesthetic sensibility, and physical beauty, the combination of which was assumed to typify the eighteenth-century woman. Philippe de Montebello, director of the Met, announced in the preface to the show's catalogue that the decisions about the contents and form of the show were Vreeland's alone, and that she "presented the eighteenth

The Met's eighteenth-century ball gown

century as it was—intimate, intriguing, and splendid," as "a time marked by extravagance and splendor in the lives of the elite." Vreeland herself explained that her show was a portrait of "the fortunate few" who "dreamed and lived and danced in one of history's most glorious periods." "These women lived in a world of promise, optimism, and possibility," Vreeland continued, in a century when "light, opportunity, and exultation were everywhere." This was a century, according to Vreeland, that "burst like a rose and spent itself lavishly" and that was "very close to the way we live today."

Like the China show, the eighteenth-century woman exhibit was

Marie Antoinette en pannier

arranged ahistorically and concentrated on surface rather than substance in its visual presentation. Upon entering, the viewer was greeted by a long, dimly lit gallery of mannequins draped in eighteenth-century costumes. The mannequins were very tall, lithe, and slinky, with pointy, robotlike bald heads either painted in gold or tightly covered in shiny metallic stockings. Avalanches of lace, silk, and ribbon work encased their slim frames, and feathers and artificial flowers sprouted from their android heads. The labels in front of the models categorized their costumes in fashion-show verbiage in the same manner used at the Chinese robes exhibit. The viewer soon became accustomed to the formulaic quality of the labels: a costume was either a "day dress," "ball gown," "evening gown," "formal gown for court presentation," "afternoon dress," or "bridal gown." Underneath the dress type was the date; dresses from different decades were clustered together. The label then described the rich stuffs of which the dress was made. A typical description: "Cloth of silver with stripes of blue silk and gold tinsel, brocaded multicolored bouquets and chinoiserie motifs, and trimmings of metallic lace and polychrome ribbon rosettes, French, about 1735."

The main costume displayed in the exhibit was the *robe en pannier*, whose silhouette billowed dramatically from a tight, slim top to a huge hooped expanse. The pannier cut packed a woman into a stiff bodice in the shape of a shield, which extended into a wide, voluminous skirt resembling a basket—hence the name "pannier." The pannier itself was a shaped metal or whalebone frame of massive hoops, on which were layered yards of material, from taffeta to silk. Some of the elaborate dresses were so wide and high that they provided the wearer with elbow rests, as was evident in the startling display "Wedding Dress of the Baroness Aelbrecht von Slingelandt" of 1759. These dresses were described by Sébastien Mercier in the eighteenth century as elaborate architectual works, whose scaffolding—the stomacher-corset and metal hoops—were prepared by the "mason," or tailor, and whose decorative façades were articulated by a special artist of ornamental surfaces, the "marchande des modes." The eighteenth-century woman was indeed a complex objet d'art, whose many surfaces were worked into a myriad of artificial manipulations. Her hair, for example, was whipped into towering dioramas, incorporating blown-glass windmills, porcelain birds, sailing ships, and farmyards complete with their animal dwellers.

Profoundly lacking in the eighteenth-century exhibition was any sense of the context in which this unbridled female luxury was situated. By lumping together costumes from many different decades in the same spaces, changes internal to fashion were obscured. More important, the singular meaning and function of fashion in eighteenth-century France were completely ignored. Fashion was inextricably linked to politics and social change in late Old Regime France; dress, and its excesses, were both the symbol of the Old Regime and the target of attack by political critics in the decades preceding the French Revolution. The weapon of philosophical reason was leveled directly against the lavishly decorated women whom Vreeland presented as "the fortunate few" who "dreamed and danced" without a care in the world.

The French Old Regime was not simply a form of political administration but a social and cultural system based on privilege and corporate hierarchy. Clothing, like every other part of social life, was charged with meaning. The outer forms of dress were not personal statements as they are today, but rather symbols of the bearer's place in the hierarchy of the three estates. Thus, knee breeches were the sign of membership in the second estate, the nobility, while only the noble men and women in attendance at the king's court could wear shoes with red leather heels. The insignias of rank and privilege continually appeared in coats of arms affixed to the surface of every possession of the noble owner, from the walls of interior spaces to the side of a woman's tiny velvet sewing kit. The welding of fashion and corporate hierarchy in the Old Regime had its most powerful testimony in the first months after the French Revolution: the noble symbol, knee breeches, was abolished, and all citizens of the nation were now to wear only trousers. The vanguard carriers of the Revolution, who replaced the logic of privilege with that of equality, were thus significantly known as the "sans-culottes"—those without breeches.

During the period of Vreeland's focus in the eighteenth-century exhibit, the period from 1720 to 1789, the rigid code governing French fashion and corporate hierarchy was undermined, with important consequences for clothing, women, and politics. The death of Louis XIV in 1714 led to the dispersing of the elite from the court of

Versailles to the city of Paris. France experienced an economic boom after 1720, which catapulted newly rich merchants, tax farmers, and financial speculators to preeminence; in record numbers these "bourgeois" of the third estate began to buy titles of nobility for entry into the second estate. The combination of economic boom, financial speculation, and noble emulation thus loosened the corporate hierarchy and led to an outburst of cultural competition: nouveaux riches bourgeois nobles, hereditary nobles, and the king, Louis XV, began vying for primacy in cultural and physical display. Part of the extravagance in dress exhibited at the Vreeland show emerged from the intensity of this intraelite competition: conspicuous consumption became the arena for combat as new groups bought their way into privilege and noble rank. Outer luxury in dress and habitat reached extraordinary proportions in the mid-eighteenth century. It was in this context that the king of France lavished one million livres per year on perfumes for his favorite, Mme. de Pompadour, and three million on her clothes; for Pompadour's successor, Mme. du Barry, Louis XV bought a bodice loaded with jewels worth five hundred thousand livres.

The competition for the monopoly on display and consumption had important consequences, which bound fashion to politics in mid-eighteenth-century France. Noble elites retreated from public life and devoted themselves to the pursuit of intimate pleasures and the refinements of interior design. As Mme. du Châtelet explained, "We now live only for agreeable and charming sensations." The catalogue for Vreeland's exhibit notes, without explanation, this withdrawal of noble elites into sybaritic abandon: "Members of society . . . were not concerned with matters of policy; their primary occupation was the pursuit of a life of wit and style—an escape from boredom at all costs."

Vreeland's exhibit and its accompanying catalogue failed to account for the profound impact that the elite cult of style and insulated indulgence had in destabilizing the Old Regime. In economic terms, as the royal treasury neared bankruptcy and suffered paralysis under the Old Regime system of privileged exemption from taxation, noble elites lavished millions of francs on overloaded physical and spatial adornments. In social terms, at the very moment that refined elites were dedicating themselves to complicated and extravagant forms of physical display and private pleasures, most of the population of France was tottering on the brink of subsistence. By the 1750s, nine out of ten French families barely survived by engaging in what the historian Olwen Hufton has called "an economy of makeshifts"; they combined rudimentary farming with seasonal migratory work. Even with this combined effort, the average family spent over half of its income on bread alone; rent and a few vegetables took care of the rest. The cult of display and the ever more opulent fashions that encased elite females in mid-century France thus operated in a context of extreme gaps between rich and poor, the haves and the have-nots. The elite immersion in extravagant outer display emphatically declared, re-stated, and extended this gap: while du Barry's bodice alone cost five hundred thousand livres, ordinary Frenchmen, on the average, barely scraped together a total of three hundred livres per year.

The glaring economic and social costs of opulence in mid-eighteenth-century France were articulated after 1750 by political critics who isolated extravagance in fashion as the key to the cor-ruption of the entire system of the Old Regime. The Enlightenment philosophers and their followers created a new political discourse in the 1760s and 1770s. They offered a set of cultural symbols as a way to attack political questions of privilege, hierarchy, power, and au-thority. These symbols turned on dress, display, and self-presentation. Thus the aristocrat was identified with luxury, idleness, effeminacy, and artificiality; the citizen, with restraint, productivity, masculinity, and authenticity. Male Roman and moral virtue was opposed to female rococo and immoral vice as the battle between liberty and privilege mounted in the pre-Revolutionary rhetoric of Diderot, Vol-taire, and Rousseau.

As in the case of the Chinese robes exhibit, Vreeland's "Eighteenth-Century Woman" obscured any issues of historical meaning and context in the service of a narcissistic project of identity. The eighteenth-century cult of luxury, the extremes of female embellish-ment, the overloaded decorated interiors—all were celebrated as indices of the taste and refinement of monied elites, as the "outburst of high living" among the wealthy, who, according to DV, are so "very close to the way we live today." Vreeland shared with La Pompadour and Marie Antoinette the impulse to an insolent denial of life outside an insulated elite; DV's declaration that her book

Allure was not tainted, that "there is no poverty here," had strange
resonances with the infamous French maxim "Let them eat cake."
The cult of emphatic distance, of visible opulence and luxury at the
moment when the gap between rich and poor was growing ever wider,
also had its parallels with the posture of the French elites. Yet lopped
from view was the outcome of this stance for its bearers: many of
the French women celebrated in Vreeland's show suffered a sorry
end on the guillotine. Indeed, a gold livery suit displayed in the
exhibit reminded us of what Vreeland strove to ignore: servants, as
in the case of that of Mme. du Barry, were known to have denounced
their mistresses and sent them off to the guillotine.

Vreeland's leveling of history into identity culminated in her peculiar presentation of the eighteenth century as a century marked by
the "power of women." The central message articulated in the show's
catalogue was the proto-modern "independence" and "force" of
eighteenth-century women, "who molded their century in their own
image." To be sure, the eighteenth century did witness the triumph of
a certain type of elite woman, like Mme. de Geoffrin, who became
the pivot of the new Enlightenment intellectual culture in the salons.
Women like de Geoffrin were celebrated in the eighteenth century
for their wit, conversation, and intellect. Vreeland's assessment of the
power of women in the eighteenth century, however, did not partake
of this Enlightenment model, valued for her linguistic virtuosity and
intellectual subtlety. The show presented evidence of the "power of
women" in ways more akin to a reassuring 1980s Reaganite fantasy:
the influence of women on men through their appearance and seduc-
tive behavior. The women isolated by Vreeland were hardly "inde-
pendent" women, but instead kept women, the dependent playthings
and showpieces of noblemen and kings. Typical of this Vreelandian
model was the favorite royal mistress of Louis XV, Mme. de Pompadour, who was celebrated for her conquest of the king and for her
subsequent influence on everything from artistic style to foreign policy.
As loving royal playmate, Pompadour was presented as assuming great
power through her proximity to and influence on the male ruler. The
way eighteenth-century women forged their power was clearly not on
the basis of ideas, but on the wily exercise of their feminine charms,
what the catalogue called their "artful maneuvers and calculated
coquetries." Vreeland's eighteenth-century women held power over

their husbands and keepers by a *force de frappe* of physical seduction and insinuation, what the catalogue called the "silken strategy" of a "force cloaked in silks, ruffles, fringes, artificial flowers, and laces." Vreeland's ideal powerful woman of the eighteenth century was most strikingly illustrated in the catalogue by the rhapsody over the "beautiful Marquise du Châtelet," a woman whose sexual power extended both to a king of France and to the Enlightenment hero Voltaire. The two illustrious men were united in their submission to a form of feminine Eros tinged with perversion.

> Visualize some of the many colorful women. . . . The Marquise du Châtelet, who read and wrote both Latin and Greek and was mistress of the beloved Voltaire. They say when she visited the king she pointed her nipples with two large rubies— much to her sovereign's delight.

The glorification of the eighteenth century as a century of "unbridled elite luxury," "hedonism," and female power in the bedroom, a distinctively Vreelandian historical transformation, resonated favorably among the insulated elite triumphant in the first year of Reaganomics. While most historians associate the extravagant fashions of the mid-eighteenth century with telling signs of the financial drain and social disparities that ultimately unraveled the Old Regime, Vreeland celebrated its fashions and females as models to be admired. The historical destiny of eighteenth-century woman was of no concern in Vreeland's logic of narcissistic historical leveling; in Vreeland's account her history just ended, with no comment, in 1789. In 1981 Bill Blass, Oscar de la Renta, and Adolfo quickly adapted their designs to evoke the elaborate ruffles and avalanched laces of the rococo Frenchwoman. Her new incarnation appeared in the diminutive and decorated frame of Nancy Reagan, whose eyelashes flicker to end consultations with her powerful husband.

Nancy Reagan's own activities between 1981 and 1982 revealed striking parallels with the insolent extravagances of the eighteenth-century women. In an economy inflicting hardship on so many, she flaunted her exercise of opulent taste. Her purchase of a $200,000 china set was only one of her more publicized projects during her early tenure as First Lady, as $41 billion was cut from the federal budget for social programs and school lunches. Her main enterprises in 1981 included the creation of a White House jewel collection and the lavish redecoration of the White House, for which she commissioned the Los Angeles "decorator of the celebrities," Ted Graber. Graber worked closely with Nancy to give the White House living quarters a "personal" quality, at a cost of $50,000 per room. The total charge for the interior redecoration was, according to Laurence Leamer, $822,641. Nancy's California friends, the Bloomingdales, Tuttles, Jorgensons, Darts, and Annenbergs, made private, tax-deductible gifts of funds to cover the decorating costs.

Architectural critic Martin Filler characterized the new Reagan White House interiors as a tasteless, "misguided sumptuary binge" whose "wall-to-wall carpeting," "brand-new Louie Schmooey gilded

The First Family bedroom (Michael Evans/The White House)

coffee tables with dark-red marble tops," and "twittery, handpainted Chinese wallpaper" emanated "the aura of nouveau riche chic." Filler explicitly contrasted the restrained grace and historical authenticity of Jacqueline Kennedy's renovations with Nancy Reagan's "California eclectic." Nancy's office phone is poised next to a framed photograph of England's Queen Mother.

Two other incidents confirmed the affinity of Nancy Reagan with Vreeland and her bevy of female aristocrats. In the spring of 1982 Mrs. Reagan was chastised by the press for her extravagant tastes and satirized as a queen with presumptive unlimited prerogatives. Annoyed by the comparison, Mrs. Reagan responded by telling reporters that she would never wear a crown—it would mess up her hair. Finally, in June 1982 the Reagans made a trip to Europe, where they visited the queen of England. The Reagans also hosted a party in Paris at the American embassy for President and Mrs. Mitterand. Nancy Reagan greeted the guests in a Galanos couture creation—a black satin tunic over rhinestone-studded black satin knickers. The enemy of the sans-culottes had now returned with a vengeance.

"High Life, Low Life, Opulence, and Delicious Hypocrisy": Vreeland's Belle Epoque Show at the Met

It was very fitting that Vreeland's historical tour of French elite opulence and female embellishment would move directly from the mid-eighteenth century to La Belle Epoque, the period ambiguously spanning 1890 to 1914. The "high living" that preceded the cataclysm of the French Revolution was now transferred to what Vreeland called the "flamboyant" and "overindulgent" life of pleasure enjoyed by elites before the explosion of World War I. As noted before, the Belle Epoque luminaries in Vreeland's newest show were themselves devoted to a revival of the mid-eighteenth century. In a period of disorienting economic, social, political, and cultural change, many members of the French elite hankered for what they imagined to be the refined *douceur de vivre* of the eighteenth century. To counteract the noisy clamor of mass politics and the menacing leveling of mass culture, French elites collected the artifacts of the eighteenth century and saw in them a vision of a world of grace, hierarchy, wit, etiquette, and exquisite femininity.

Nancy Reagan in a Chinese robe (Newsweek—John Ficara)

Vreeland's "La Belle Epoque," which opened on December 12, 1982, did not refer to the self-conscious and defensive association that 1890s elites cultivated with the eighteenth century. Her show presented upper-class women in their splendid clothes as emblems of the continuity of the great French couturier tradition, triumphant in the eighteenth century, and of the aristocratic woman as objet d'art that this tradition was established to serve. The couturiers represented in the show included Worth, Pacquin, Doucet, Poiret, and Redfurn. The illustrious women gracing their creations were featured in the Met show—the Comtesse Greffulhe, the Marquise Boni de Castellane, Queen Alexandra and Queen Victoria of England, the Duchess of Marlborough, the Comtesse Anna de Noailles, and the Duchesse de Broglie.

Vreeland's Belle Epoque offered the public a vision of a frivolous, flamboyant elite dedicated to a life of pleasure, leisure, and luxury. "The mood was buoyant, ebullient, and delicious," exclaimed Vreeland in her taped tour through the show; "it was a time devoted to the pursuit of the best of everything; music was everywhere." There was an attempt to reproduce this musical surround, for the spectator entering the gallery was immediately bombarded with piped-in music typifying the Gay Nineties: "Ta-ra-ra-boom-tee-ay" alternated with Strauss waltzes in endless repetition. The music served as an accompaniment in the entry gallery to a dark set re-creating Maxim's, the classy bar and restaurant originally built in the 1890s and now owned by Pierre Cardin, the sponsor of the Vreeland Met show. A huge painted mural depicting the "Bar at Maxim's" by Galland provided the backdrop for the first gallery of fashions. The center of Galland's painting caught an encounter between a well-dressed gentleman in evening wear and a woman bent over the bar counter in a suggestive diaphanous costume. The woman's posture, the fit of her dress, and her exposed black-stockinged foot were all signs of her availability for hire. The mural magnified the "Bar at Maxim's" as the site of high-class Belle Epoque sexual solicitation.

Vreeland's Met mannequins were posed in front of the Galland mural as if they had just stepped out of the bar. The lavish costumes appropriate for an evening at Maxim's—elaborate layers of lace, fur, velvet, and silk—were draped over the now familiar Vreeland mannequins with painted gold or stocking-covered heads and unmarked robot faces. As in the previous exhibits, the explanation of the costumes was limited to labels of fashion-show jargon; the information included a statement of the rich stuffs of which the costume was made, the name of its designer, and the name of its original wearer. The spectator was greeted with a panoply of dazzling outfits, shining out from the gold mannequin frames in the red Maxim's gallery. Among them was an "evening jacket, of green velvet trim with embroidered arabesques, worn by the Princesse Viggo, created by Worth in 1896."

Extending the theme of the eighteenth-century woman, the Belle Epoque show celebrated woman as a privileged decorative and sexual object. Vreeland presented the Belle Epoque woman as "an elegant and graceful creature" whose goal was to be seen and to "overwhelm and silence her rivals," what Vreeland called the "standard form of female one-upmanship." This was a woman, according to DV, whose "elaborate rows of ruffled petticoats were changed constantly, by maids of the house whose sole job was to change ruffles." In the other galleries that made up the exhibit, women in couturier ensembles were displayed lounging in waves of white lace for "summer days in the garden," and were arranged in two "ceremonial rooms" in ball gowns and court dresses. As in the other shows, the women were surrounded with the accessories and interior decor typical of the period. Thus 1890s painted fans, shoes and shoe trunks, Art Nouveau vases and jewelry, and screens and posters complemented the costumes, whose serpentine floral designs often echoed the shapes of the Art Nouveau organic decor. The composite image conveyed of the Belle Epoque woman was as an exquisite ornament, whose frame was packed into a tight corset and bustle. If the eighteenth-century woman extended sideways in vast hooped panniers, the Belle Epoque woman was bustled back into a train, appearing from the front as a svelte, encased hourglass.

The decorative and sexy Belle Epoque female of Vreeland's rendering mingled aristocratic pedigree with demimondaine raciness. Following the selective strategy exemplified in the eighteenth-century show, Vreeland presented the Belle Epoque woman as a wife or mistress of a king or aristocrat. The demimonde, the half world of actresses, dancers, and courtesans that was frequented by illustrious men, fascinated Vreeland. The "great courtesans" of the Belle

Epoque—Cléo de Mérode, Lillie Langtry, La Belle Otéro, and the actress Sarah Bernhardt—appeared, in their couturier outfits and splendid accessories, side by side with the queens and countesses of Europe. The demimondaine conquests of kings, noblemen, financiers, and journalists were well chronicled in the gossipy catalogue prepared by Philippe Julien.

As in the "Chinese Robes" and "Eighteenth-Century Woman" exhibitions, the visual strategy and selectivity deployed by Vreeland in "La Belle Epoque" effected a fundamental contextual leveling; historical meaning and substance were eliminated in a narcissistic project of identity. Eager to portray the elites of the past as pleasure-seeking predecessors to the Reagan clan, Vreeland promoted the Belle Epoque as a "glamorous period, full of laughter and fun, marked by lots of noise, lots of romance, and *great* style." It was an enviable time when, noted the catalogue, "people had confidence in cash," and when a "stylish aristocracy helped to make the world a little more amusing and much less ugly."

The image of the Belle Epoque as a carefree, frothy era when stylish elites engaged in a perpetual cancan had little relation to historical reality. Indeed, the very term "Belle Epoque," and the fun-filled romp it connoted, were the nostalgic invention of a later generation. After World War I, Europeans projected, retrospectively, a myth of the late nineteenth century as a glittering, halcyon era when innocence and spectacle reigned supreme. Yet the sybaritic "banquet years," the bubbly and naughty Belle Epoque, existed in large part only in the shattered imaginations of postwar society.

The elites who actually experienced the 1890s, however, did not consider themselves to be living in a golden "belle époque." Their own term for the waning nineteenth century was the more pessimistic "fin de siècle," which conveyed the fear of decline, degeneration, and decadence that educated Europeans sensed was spreading throughout their societies at a menacing pace. A fundamental ambivalence to modernity marked the European elite at the century's turn. Political turbulence, economic change, social dislocation, and cultural crisis altered the landscape of European society and created unprecedented problems for the ruling and governing classes. The extension of universal suffrage and parliamentary government realized the liberal dream while it also yielded the nightmare of the mass, and of chauvinist nationalism and anti-Semitism as powerful, irrational political forces. In France the antiparliamentarist nationalism of General Boulanger, and the virulent anti-Semitism fueling the Dreyfus affair, rocked the republic in the 1890s. The Dreyfus affair in particular divided families and ruined friendships within the fin-de-siècle French elite. The consolidation of the city as a mass metropolis expanded the possibilities for lavish entertainments while it also gave birth to agoraphobia—a fear of wide-open spaces, which became something of an epidemic as the century waned. Many strollers in Paris and Vienna found themselves paralyzed at the prospect of crossing the street—a vast boulevard, where horse-drawn carriages, omnibuses, and hurried pedestrians maneuvered together. Parisian dwellers were startled by the encroachment of a technological monument on the city skyline—the thousand-foot Eiffel Tower. Protesters against the wrought-iron tower saw it as "an odious factory spire," the sign of an "American Babylon of the future," the unavoidable symbol of a new rationalized and standardized modernity that threatened the individual with anonymity and insignificance. Fin-de-siècle elites were also disturbed by the revelations of a new psychology, which subverted assumptions about the nature of reality and how it was perceived. By the time Sigmund Freud arrived in Paris in 1885, the discoveries of his French mentor, Dr. Jean-Martin Charcot, were widely debated by politicians, journalists, and legal magistrates. Charcot's experiments with hypnosis, suggestion, and hysteria had implications for everything from free will to crowd behavior. The primacy of mind as a rational Cartesian grid was now challenged by the exposure of mind as a fluid, febrile chamber, susceptible to images and suggestive forces. One pathology connected with the new psychology, neurasthenia, afflicted many members of the Belle Epoque elite. A condition of nervous exhaustion, neurasthenia was marked by listlessness and fatigue; it was assumed to result from the overexertion wrought by the stress and strain of modern urban life. Thus Vreeland's Belle Epoque elite confronted unprecedented and disorienting problems. They were more riven and driven, and less "innocent and naughty," than Vreeland allows us to understand. These extravagant high-livers sought refuge in pleasure from the external menace of the iron cage, only to be greeted by the unsettling instability of the inner world of the psyche.

The multiple problems of the fin de siècle resonated in the contents of the Vreeland show, though they eluded explicit mention. Many of the applied arts and posters displayed as "authentic" backdrops to the costume exhibits expressed the political conflicts of the late century. Emile Gallé, the Art Nouveau glassmaker from Nancy, inscribed the surface of his vases with the thorny French "warrior" thistle and with nationalist slogans proclaiming France's ultimate revenge against Germany for the 1870 annexation of Lorraine. The power of nationalism in late-century politics emerged again in a poster of Maude Adams as Joan of Arc, a heroine who became a cult figure in the French nationalist movement of the early years of the twentieth century. The impact of the Dreyfus affair also made its mark on the exhibit. Gallé, though a strident nationalist, was also an ardent defender of Captain Dreyfus, and worked for the acquittal of the Jewish officer against the army that condemned him. Some of the Gallé vases displayed in the Vreeland show were conceived as visual propaganda on Dreyfus's behalf. "If justice is not done, let all my glass shatter to bits"—this Gallé carved along the surface of his vases during the period of Dreyfus's retrial. An alternative position on the Dreyfus affair, and the poisonous anti-Semitism infusing it, was evident in the work of another artist included at the show: the caricaturist Georges Goursat, also known as Sem. A series of Sem's color lithographs of high society life were exhibited next to the "Bar at Maxim's," in the entryway gallery displaying evening fashion. In many prints Sem visualized, in blunt and exaggerated lines, the stereotypically Semitic features of influential Jews, including the Baron Alphonse de Rothschild, Raoul Ginsbourg, and Marcel Ephrussi. Sem's elite anti-Semitism received confirmation in the broadsheets depicting hook-nosed Dreyfus as the traitor Jew poisoning France.

Fin-de-siècle politics and psychology converged at the Vreeland show in the pervasive presence of Marcel Proust. Vreeland's "La Belle Epoque" was really a tribute to her favorite author; she considered the Belle Epoque quintessentially "Proustian" and modeled her displays on the illustrious figures from Proust's own social set and that of his novels. Thus Vreeland concentrated on the exquisite finery worn by the Comtesse Greffulhe, described in the show's taped guide as the primary object of Proust's adoration and the model for his Duchesse de Guermantes. Vreeland reconstructed the bird-of-paradise hat and dress ensemble worn by the comtesse, on which Proust lavished pages of intricate description in *The Guermantes Way*. In close proximity to the outfits of the comtesse hung a large Boldini portrait of the Comte Robert de Montesquiou-Fézensac, described in the tape as the comtesse's cousin, as Proust's close friend, and as the model for the Baron de Charlus in his novels. Other Proustian figures received Vreeland's attention: a portrait and evening dress of Sarah Bernhardt, the actress worshipped by Proust, were exhibited in the ceremonial room. Near the divine Sarah were the clothes and portrait of Proust's lifelong friend and patron, the Comtesse Anna de Noailles.

Vreeland admired Proust for his impeccable social skills and for his manifold aristocratic connections. Yet her presentation of Proust missed the fundamental principle guiding his vision and his novels: irony. Proust treated his illustrious aristocratic figures with devastating sarcasm and corrosive irony. While he aspired to penetrate the inner sanctum of aristocratic society, he realized, upon arrival, that it was a hollow world full of cruelty and stupidity. The figures lovingly re-created by Vreeland as a tribute to Proust's objects of desire were the very figures he recast into deadly parodies: the Duchesse de Guermantes and the Baron de Charlus are, in Proust's rendering, affected, perverse, boring, empty, and ultimately comic figures. In her own obsessive hankering for social distinction and aristocratic cachet, Vreeland transformed Proust from detached social critic to starry-eyed socialite. Politics deeply affected the aesthete writer, who chronicled the divisive social impact of the Dreyfus affair in his *Cities of the Plain*. The psychology of neurasthenia and suggestion also played its part in Proust's life and work. Yet such things were excluded from Vreeland's view. As she could re-create an entire historical period in the image of 1980s opulence, so too could she press Marcel Proust into the service of her unbridled aristocratic wish-fulfillment. Rather than the ironic, anxious misfit, fated to live out the contradictions of his Jewishness and his social ambitions, Proust was rediscovered as an admirable snob and sybarite. Vreeland's presentation had as little to do with the real Proust as did her representation of the stylish Belle Epoque elite who never left Maxim's with the real society of that era.

If the external conflicts confounding the fin de siècle were central missing links in the Vreeland exhibit, changes more intrinsic to fashion itself also surfaced in it, though they too were left un-

The Comtesse Greffulhe, Proust's "Duchesse de Guermantes"

explained. For if fashion was indivisible from politics in pre-Revolutionary France, it was directly associated with social and cultural crisis in fin-de-siècle France. Changing assumptions about the nature of women and economic transformations in the clothing industry altered the look, fit, and function of clothes in the late nineteenth century and disrupted the perceptual categories applied to visual appearance.

Fin-de-siècle Frenchmen were haunted by the specter of the *femme nouvelle*, the "New Woman," who left home and family for education and a career. The passage of the divorce law of 1884, the emergence of a French feminist movement, and the expansion of higher education for women in the late century created a new visibility for women and shaped a widespread public awareness of female mobility. The actual number of French women affected by these changes was small. Yet the public and unfamiliar character of a new type of bourgeois woman generated a powerful symbol of the New Woman. In fin-de-siècle French newspapers and caricature magazines, the New Woman was alternately envisioned as a gargantuan amazon or a severe, frock-coated masculine female. The sturdy virago was depicted as rejecting the norm of female bourgeois domesticity and as threatening to dislocate the essential divisions that ordered bourgeois life: public from private, work from family, production from reproduction. In a period when French politicians worried over the military implications of the declining French birthrate, the childless New Woman was associated with a threat to national security. One contemporary commentator summarized what a woman should be, in contrast to the horror of the New Woman, in 1896:

> A woman is a being apart . . . endowed by nature with other functions than the man with whom she has no business competing in public life. A woman exists only through her ovaries.

The mobile New Woman was linked in the late century with a new technological device, the metallic bicycle. The amazon was depicted in cartoons as a husband-heckling shrew who made her way to feminist congresses dressed in pantaloons, astride a shiny bicycle. The fashion for cycling appeared in the Vreeland show: Vreeland casually mentioned that the bicycle promoted a new line of *sportif* clothes for women. Yet the fin-de-siècle linkage of the menacing New Woman and the bicycle, and the controversy provoked by women's donning "androgynous" outfits for cycling, were lost from the Vreelandian view. At a time when women were encased in corsets and wrapped in layers of petticoats, the practical cycling wear signaled a change in more than fashion. It was inseparable from the disorienting perception that women were breaking out of their gilded cages.

If Belle Epoque French fashion was related to the problem of the New Woman, fashion was also enmeshed in a fundamental economic transformation, which had social and cultural consequences. Vreeland's exclusive display of *couturier* fashion obscured the profound challenge posed to the individual designer by the new commercial expansion of the clothing industry. Indeed, by the 1890s a full-scale revolution in fashion was under way, which consolidated the economy and production of the clothing industry as we know it today. The arrival of the department store in mid-century expanded the market and democratized fashion. Rather than the specialized handiwork of the couturier, the department store's need for volume, rapid turnover, and lower cost fostered a new type of fashion: ready-to-wear. Ready-to-wear fashions imitated the look and designs of the individual couturiers while widely disseminating clothing styles in fashion pattern books and in mail-order catalogues. This commercialization and democratization of fashion startled many fin-de-siècle Frenchmen; it subverted the capacity to categorize the position of the wearer on the social scale by clothing type. One commentator in 1891 claimed that the signs of distinction had thus shifted from outer to inner layers: in a period of department-store leveling, only the quality and number of petticoats, corsets, and underwear could distinguish a woman from her social inferiors. Particularly irksome to some contemporary Frenchmen was the inability to differentiate elite women from prostitutes. Octave Uzanne, a fin-de-siècle writer, claimed that the equalizing effect of ready-to-wear clothing made it impossible to know whether it was the prostitutes or the aristocratic women who were setting the tone for fashion. In the new and rapid rhythm of fashion fads generated by department-store novelty, it was unclear who was keeping up with whom.

Vreeland concentrated on couturier fashion as if the individual dressmaker had been left untouched by the commercial and cultural revolution effected by department store ready-to-wear. In addition, she seemed to share, though without worry, the confusion between prostitutes and aristocrats that perplexed fin-de-siècle contemporaries. In representing the Belle Epoque as a world of perpetual leisure and pleasure, Vreeland never mentioned that nighttime leisure separated most men from their wives. The naughty nightlife of Maxim's was the preserve of upper-bourgeois and aristocratic men entertained by their mistresses, the courtesans of the demimonde, whose liaisons were illustrated by the Galland mural. Bourgeois and aristocratic wives never accompanied their husbands to the club; this was a world with discrete compartments for different types of women: wives serving husbands at home and demimondaines catering to lovers at Maxim's. Vreeland collapsed the courtesans and the illustrious wives together. Her Maxim's costume gallery displayed evening fashion for noble and wealthy bourgeois women, as well as for the courtesans, as they all would have appeared at Maxim's. Yet the Comtesse Greffulhe was not a frequenter of Maxim's; Sarah Bernhardt and Cléo de Mérode were. Vreeland screened out this historical feature and projected instead a fantastic commingling of matrons and prostitutes in a universe of pleasure.

The unity of women, money, and power did characterize a gala evening of a more contemporary elite: the extravagant party that inaugurated the Vreeland "Belle Epoque" show at the Met. Pierre Cardin sponsored the lavish event of December 9, 1982, with social chairwoman Mrs. William Buckley. Cardin prepared for the one evening of the party a striking reconstruction of the bar at Maxim's, whose original Art Nouveau decor he had bought and was in the process of transferring to a new location. The reconstituted Maxim's (at a cost of $500,000) provided a canopy for Cristina DeLorean, Nancy Kissinger, Betsy Bloomingdale, and 750 socialites, politicians, fashion designers, and movie stars who paid $500 each to parade their own opulent outfits, to dine on cold beef stuffed with pâté de foie gras, and to dance to the live orchestra playing the same Strauss waltzes and cancans piped in at the costume show. The *New York Times* commented that the partygoers of 1982 simulated the qualities—"opulence and vulgarity, delicious hypocrisy and innocent naughtiness"—attributed to the Belle Epoque elite by Vreeland. Yet as these qualities were only the ahistorical projections of Vreelandian fantasies about the 1890s, so too they belied the experience of the 1980s jet set. The Cardin extravaganza provided a third occasion, following the spectacles inaugurating the "Chinese Robes" and "Eighteenth-Century Woman" shows, for a public glorification of opulence in the image of a resurrected aristocracy of privilege and license.

Bloomingdale's "Fête de France": The Consumerist "Celebration of French Creativity and Style"

As the Vreeland "Belle Epoque" exhibit closed its doors in September 1983, Bloomingdale's displayed the fruits of an extravagant marketing campaign dedicated to French opulence and elegance. The splendid Met array of accessories and couturier outfits that had embellished eighteenth- and nineteenth-century aristocratic French women, turning them into elaborate objets d'art, were now reprocessed, in consumer volume, for trendy New York shoppers. The alliance between museum exhibition and commercial exploitation manifested in the chinoiseries of 1980–81 was now transposed to elite Francophilia.

On September 18, 1983, Bloomingdale's proclaimed a "romance in full bloom" with France in a "dazzling salute to French products and culture." The Bloomingdale's "Fête de France" aspired to re-create the essence of France within the walls of the department store. The Lexington Avenue premises were given over to French designers, who, with the aid of East Side store managers, reconstituted the authentic "atmosphere of shops, galleries, salons, and bistros." Shop stalls and entire Parisian streets brimming with crystal, pottery, linens, perfumes, food, and wine sprang up on the New York site. These quintessential products of France were accompanied by their creators, who were transported to Bloomingdale's for live demonstrations. Chefs of one-, two-, and three-star restaurants, designer couturiers, lace makers, embroiderers, textile engravers, glass blowers, silversmiths, interior decorators, and furniture craftsmen all practiced their skills and peddled their wares in midtown. According to Bloomingdale's promotion literature, these craftsmen displayed the sensibilities that have always distinguished the ineffable *"cachet français."* The France represented at Bloomingdale's, and advertised in its brochures, was the country devoted to "the art of living well," to the cult of "personal

FÊTE · DE · FRANCE

A CELEBRATION OF FRENCH CREATIVITY AND STYLE

From today till November 6, Bloomingdale's will celebrate a romance with France that began a century ago, with our first trips to see and to buy. Today, the romance blooms into a true love affair.

Far more than a display of merchandise, Fête de France is a cultural festival on the grand scale, a feast for all the senses, where you can see, hear, taste and feel the sophistication of Paris or the charm of an inn in France of the past, present and future.

In all of the Bloomingdale's stores you will find priceless sculptures and paintings from the museums of France... evocations of the symbols of Paris—the famed Normandie, the Statue of Liberty, The Eiffel Tower, films and videotapes of the legends of Piaf, Chevalier and Bardot.

Artisans, craftspeople and the great chefs of France will bring the taste and touch of French skill to life. France of the future will be reflected in the technological displays of aerospace, flight, computer and satellite expertise.

Streets of shops from Paris to Provence, model rooms by famous French interior designers, the Artcurial gallery, a parfumerie, the restaurant L'Ecluse, a French newstand—every aspect of France is recreated.

And fashion, the signature of France, as seen by the well known and the new designers in shops and fashion events—will continue the traditions.

The richness of France's heritage, the dynamics of today, the challenge of the future, here at Bloomingdale's. Celebrate with us this Fête de France.

September 13 — November 6

bloomingdale's

New York, Boston, Washington, Philadelphia, Dallas (premiering October 10th).

Bloomingdale's 1983 "Fête de France"

79

pleasures," and to the infusion of elegance and "passionate aesthetics" in all arenas of daily life. The lessons to be learned from these French imports and their purchase was, as one Bloomingdale's spokesman noted, that "living well is an art well worth the cultivation."

As in the Met shows, the French essence celebrated at Bloomingdale's was artisanal, aristocratic, and intimate. The France reconstituted on Lexington Avenue was not the country of Mitterrand or, for that matter, of ordinary Frenchmen, but rather the domain of the three absolutist kings Louis and their refined aristocratic cohorts. It was not the country that trumpeted liberty, equality, and fraternity, but the palace from which rang *"Après moi le déluge"* and "Let them eat cake." It was not the country that spawned the Rights of Man and Citizen, but the civilization devoted to the delights of woman and the aristocracy of the spirit. Finally, Bloomingdale's France was not the France of Enlightenment and common sense admired by Tom Paine, Thomas Jefferson, and Benjamin Franklin, but the France idealized by elitist culture vultures and affluent parvenus: the condenser of privilege, distinction, and the life filled with exquisite elegance bequeathed by the Old Regime aristocracy to their self-appointed spiritual heirs in the modern period.

This aristocratic bias appeared consistently in Bloomingdale's ads and promotion literature for the fete. The announcement brochure, a supplement to the *New York Times* on September 18, emphasized cultural and aesthetic endowments as the timeless qualities of France. The gifts of delicacy, grace, and the art of living were elementally French, transcending the vicissitudes of politics and history. The purveyors of these national talents were the great French artisans, associated explicitly by Bloomingdale's with the royal and aristocratic systems they had originally served. Among the main attractions at the Fête de France was the glassware of Baccarat, advertised as "Baccarat, Crystal of Kings," whose "elegance and timeless beauty has graced tables of royalty for centuries" and "is still the crystal connoisseur's choice today." Baccarat designed, exclusively for Bloomingdale's, a crystal paperweight in the shape of the fleur-de-lis, the insignia of the Bourbon kings, which has been banished from the French flag and official residences since the Revolution. Complementing the Baccarat displays were silver items by Christofle, described in the ads as "haute couture pour la table," whose silversmiths "have furnished many a palace"; lace works, originally "royal and noble adornments" worn by "men and women of high station . . . as an expression of their superior rank"; Limoges china, whose exquisite quality emerged during the reign of Louis XV; Boucheron "jewelry of exceptional splendor" by the "jewelry originators for the crowned heads of the world"; and the sumptuous "Parfums Caron Montaigne," dispensed from Louis XV Baccarat crystal urns, so loved by aristocrats that one of them, Mme. de Pompadour, "spent the equivalent of a million dollars a year on scents." All of these luxury items, identified as the historical accoutrements of aristocratic privilege, were offered for sale en masse to Bloomingdale's consumers. The message suggested by these descriptions and craft products was that the legacies of refinement and elegance, nurtured by French kings and nobles, might rub off on the children of American democracy. Gentrified New York buyers, buoyed by the deluge of elite French style at the Met, could now find salvation by association with the artifacts of a life once lived in splendor, insulation, and quality unsurpassed.

A la Recherche d'Argent Perdu: Vreeland's "Yves Saint Laurent" at the Met, 1983–1984

Follow Yves down the garden path, there's
always a pot of gold at the end.
                              —Diana Vreeland, 1983

One week after the Bloomingdale's Fête de France ended, the Metropolitan Museum opened the doors of the Costume Institute to another installment of Vreelandian extravagance. On December 12, 1983, Vreeland moved from luxury wrapped in historical clothing to a celebration of contemporary French elegance: "Twenty-Five Years of Yves Saint Laurent." In this tribute to a living French fashion designer, the high culture and consumer versions of Francophile opulence came together. For Saint Laurent is both the "dauphin" of exclusive female splendor and the czar of a global fashion empire devoted to designer mass marketing.

Besides presenting Saint Laurent as the inheritor of the great tradition of the couturier celebrated in the two previous exhibits, this exhibit extended the narcissistic image making that Vreeland practiced

in all of the costume shows. As has been noted, the "Chinese Robes,"
"Eighteenth-Century Woman," and "Belle Epoque" exhibitions were
all indelibly stamped with the Vreelandian preference for the "far-
fetched fantasy" over "fact"; in all these shows Vreeland remade
history in the image of the opulence, luxury, and social privilege of
the Reaganite elites in the 1980s. Vreeland's Saint Laurent exhibit
at the Met dropped the historical dressing for aristocratic license
altogether: the show was a literal mirror held up to the affluent stratum

Saint Laurent with Met mannequins, 1983

of 1980s society. Previous displays of the lavish costumes of Chinese empresses, Mme. de Pompadour, and Comtesse Greffulhe now gave way to the finery worn by a contemporary elite clientele, among them Diana Vreeland herself, the Comtesse von Bülow, Mrs. Edgar Chrysler, and Pauline de Rothschild.

Diana Vreeland's association with Saint Laurent dated back to the late 1950s, when, as a columnist for *Vogue*, she had celebrated the "charm" and "languor" of the young Frenchman's designs. Saint Laurent had been present, in one way or another, in all of the Met costume shows organized by Vreeland. The Chinese robes in 1980 were steeped in YSL's Opium perfume. And many of the shimmering costumes worn by the guests at the gala parties inaugurating the three Met exhibitions were haute couture creations by Yves Saint Laurent. A show exclusively dedicated to the seer of French fashion was thus a fitting addition, forming a triptych of French elegance from the eighteenth century to the present.

The Saint Laurent retrospective at the Met recapitulated the themes of all the Vreeland shows, celebrating as it did elite opulence and visualizing a world of permanent leisure and privilege without responsibility. It promoted the continuity between the modern elite and the lavish nobility displayed at previous Vreeland exhibits. The entryway gallery, devoted to a display of sumptuous evening clothes, announced the affinity between the bearers of style today and their noble predecessors. Spectators crossed the threshold into the Costume Institute and were greeted by a familiar row of sightless gold manne-quins, disposed across the same dimly lit room. This time the manne-quins' rococo finery and Belle Epoque voluptuousness were replaced by Saint Laurent black evening outfits. "Evening overblouse of black silk chiffon with silk sleeves, trimmed with black satin ribbon, Spring/Summer 1962"; "Black evening jacket with sable trim, over black silk blouse trimmed with gold and silver sequins, Fall/Winter, 1972–73"; "Black tulle evening gown, embroidered with jet and ostrich feathers, Fall/Winter 1982–83": these were some of the en-sembles displayed. These models were set against a large mural that composed a huge backdrop for the entire room. Decorators had blown up to wall size an eighteenth-century engraving of a splendid noble palace. In the foreground of the print stood a male courtier, con-versing with a lovely lady in pannier-hooped skirts underneath a

The Met's Saint Laurent evening suit

cartouche emblazoned with a noble coat of arms. Behind the dashing couple a series of arches echoed back into space, offering a trompe-l'oeil perspective into the distant recesses of the palace. The gilded mannequins in Saint Laurent clothing were placed in front of the magnified backdrop in such a way as to appear to be emerging from the perspective arches. The resulting relationship between manne-quins and wall mural suggested that the Saint Laurent beauties had walked directly out of the picture plane and into our view. This clever device captured the theme of the essential continuity between the Saint Laurent couturier ensembles and the haute couture outfits dis-played at the previous French shows, between the contemporary affluent elite dressed by Saint Laurent and the stylish aristocracy garbed by the great couturiers of the eighteenth century and the Belle Epoque. The message proclaimed at the Saint Laurent entryway was that elegance, "allure," and social privilege have continued, un-abated, from the eighteenth century to the present.

The affinity between the Saint Laurent exhibit and the previous Vreeland shows continued as the retrospective unfolded. The social link between the Saint Laurent clientele and the Vreelandian no-bilities of the past emerged in the reappearance of some of the same French families that had figured in "The Eighteenth-Century Woman" and "La Belle Epoque." Peppered throughout the Saint Laurent exhi-bition were the evening dresses worn by the Baroness Alain de Roths-child in 1972 and by the wife of the Baron Philippe de Rothschild in 1983, and the thigh-high brown suede boots commissioned by Pauline de Rothschild in 1963. Another member of the French nobility was featured in the Saint Laurent show, testifying to the continuity of generations of haute couture and allure: the Duchesse d'Orléans. A gold mannequin draped in a silk and satin wedding dress, with a veil of white tulle and lace, appeared in the very place where the Belle Epoque show had displayed a mannequin wearing the wedding dress of the Comtesse Greffulhe. The label at the Saint Laurent exhibit read, "Wedding dress . . . worn by H.R.H. Madame la Duchesse d'Orléans in 1969." Her Royal Highness's family have been aspirants to the French crown for over a century.

The continuity between the Saint Laurent show and the preceding Vreeland exhibits emerged further in the explicit "quotation" of previ-ous material. The lavish costumes of all three prior exhibits were used

The Met's Saint Laurent wedding gown for
"H.R.H. Madame la Duchesse d'Orléans"

by Saint Laurent as inspirations for his own fashions, and his historical reinventions of Chinese and French aristocracies were prominently displayed. One room featured "chinoiseries"—lavish costumes modeled on imperial Chinese robes and the silhouettes of Chinese pagodas. One of these "Chinese evening ensembles" included a strange mingling of elite and popular themes. A Chinese "jacket of black silk gazar embroidered with gold oak leaves over a dress of black satin crepe," inspired by the sumptuous embellishment of imperial Chinese robes, was accompanied by "a coolie hat, gold lamé, lined and trimmed with mink." This ensemble, which was part of Diana Vreeland's personal wardrobe, was lent by her to the show. In the Chinese robes show, Vreeland had suggested the existence of a world outside the Chinese imperial court in a single figure: a short mannequin dressed in a white robe and a simple straw coolie hat. Now the coolie hat had reappeared, mink-lined, as an accessory to the bizarre chinoiserie imagined by Yves Saint Laurent.

In addition to the Chinese themes, there were also links between the Saint Laurent and the previous French shows. The pannier hoops of eighteenth-century rococo fashion reappeared in Saint Laurent's trapeze dresses of the late 1950s and in more recent gowns expanding outlandishly sideways. The fashions and mood of La Belle Epoque also made their mark on the Saint Laurent show, indicating the designer's own fascination with the world of Proust. A "Belle Epoque" wedding dress, made of beige organdy shot with gold, echoed the shape and silhouette typical of the late nineteenth century. The dress had mutton sleeves and a layered bustle, and was worn with a matching face veil, small hat, and hand-embroidered parasol. This ensemble could have gone unnoticed among the svelte hourglass fashions at the Vreeland tribute to the 1890s. A series of white lace blouses and long skirts also mirrored outfits exhibited at the "Belle Epoque" show.

Saint Laurent himself offered some interesting comments in the exhibition's catalogue, and in press interviews, concerning the continuity of haute couture and the female aristocracy of the spirit that promotes it in the modern world. Saint Laurent was catapulted to the center of international haute couture by his association, from age nineteen, with the house of Dior. When Christian Dior died suddenly in 1957, Yves Saint Laurent, at twenty-one, was appointed head

The Met's Saint Laurent chinoiseries

designer. After a dispute with the house of Dior in 1960, the young prodigy set up his own haute couture establishment, with the financial backing of an American businessman from Atlanta. Until 1966 Saint Laurent flourished as an haute couture designer, creating lavish clothes celebrated in the international high fashion community for their subtlety and finish. Yet by 1966 he confronted a fundamental threat to the haute couture enterprise. The 1960s counterculture challenged

The Met's Saint Laurent Belle Epoque wedding gown

the premise of elitist, expensive, and outlandish clothes for women and undercut the demand for houte couture even among Saint Laurent's own clientele. Diana Vreeland herself was a casualty of this challenge to haute couture—in 1971 she was fired from the editorship of *Vogue* owing to the sense that her promotion of lavish haute couture outfits, including those by Saint Laurent, was out of sync with the new political culture and the changing desires of the *Vogue* buying public.

In addition to the impact of the sixties on fashion, Saint Laurent was plagued by the same commercial and marketing pressures that had originally menaced the haute couturiers of the 1890s. Unlike his predecessors, he was better equipped to adapt to the necessities of mass marketing. In 1966 he established an addition to his haute couture line that resolved the challenge of the mass market: ready-to-wear Saint Laurent fashions, produced in volume for commercial boutiques. In tandem with the ready-to-wear clothes, Saint Laurent cashed in on another merchandising invention: he licensed companies to use his name on perfume, scarves, handbags, and cosmetics. It was only the addition of the machine-made *prêt-à-porter* clothes for international commerce, and the retail licensees, that enabled Saint Laurent to survive. Indeed, the ready-to-wear boutiques and licensing proceeds have subsidized the Saint Laurent haute couture operations since the late 1960s. The underwriting of the mass market ensured the continuation of the unique and expensive handmade designs of the couturier.

Paradoxically, the Vreeland exhibition celebrated Saint Laurent as an haute couture artist, obscuring the dialectic between exclusive design and mass merchandising at the heart of his success. Saint Laurent welcomed the Met show as the triumphant return of haute couture into the public mainstream. Whereas the sixties had forced haute couture underground, the eighties brought luxury back into the spotlight. The opulent couture fashion, and the customers who could afford it among the Reaganite elite, were now, ironically, characterized as the "return of the repressed."

Saint Laurent expressed his delight at the haute couture focus of the Met show in terms of an aristocratic disdain for marketing democratization. In a *New York Times* interview he explained that the exhibit inaugurated his new focus, to "re-create the immense prestige and the immense luxury of the 1950s," the period of the greatest success of his haute couture design. In the Met exhibition catalogue, reprinted in *New York* magazine, Saint Laurent described his work by evoking the pre-Revolutionary traditions of couture as a "noble" craft, which had to be guarded, through the taste and refinement of a small group, from the "derogation" it would suffer from the mass:

> Dior taught me to love something other than fashion and style: the essential nobility of a couturier's craft. . . . The couture began as a place where the most knowledgeable and most exigent of women were dressed with the greatest perfection. It survives because a few of those women still survive. . . . I believe that the couture must be preserved at all costs, and the term, like a title, protected from debasement. Haute couture has its multitudes of whispered secrets that a small number of people are still able to pass on. . . . I, because of luck and instinct, am one of the last to hold the secrets of haute couture.

Vreeland's Saint Laurent presentation reiterated the essential link between historical and contemporary luxury, organizing the Saint Laurent costumes along a single axis—leisure. Following exactly the order of the suite of rooms used in the preceding French shows, the Saint Laurent fashions were arranged according to their varied functions in a life of permanent pleasure. The entry gallery that had most recently re-created the outfits of the Belle Epoque high-livers at Maxim's was now replaced with the elegant "evening-wear" of Saint Laurent's couture customers. The rooms behind the "evening-wear" were devoted to daytime social distractions. The site where Belle Epoque ladies had lounged in lace for teatime in the garden was now inhabited by contemporary elegant females lolling, strolling, and visiting in the park. A glittering "red room" completed the continuity of the Saint Laurent exhibitions with previous Vreeland visions of fashion in the service of uninterrupted diversion. The Saint Laurent "red room" replaced the "ceremonial room" of the "Belle Epoque" exhibit, in which the lavish finery of the Comtesse Greffulhe, Queen Alexandra, and Sarah Bernhardt had dazzled over 500,000 visitors. It displayed Saint Laurent's most outlandish and theatrical costumes for evening wear, among them the Chinese evening ensembles, a series of long skirts, gold headdresses, and ornate bodices and blouses inspired by Russian peasants, and a number of "Spanish" fashions, which piled layers of gold on mannequins so that they resembled gilded matadors. These were the types of evening clothes destined to make a real splash at a gala social event, and designed, as Vreeland had said the clothes from the Belle Epoque were designed, to "overwhelm and silence a woman's rivals."

In an echo of the other shows, Vreeland organized the Saint Laurent show ahistorically, telescoping three decades of Saint Laurent's production into a series of formal, "primordial" fashion ideas. Rather than being arranged chronologically, the Saint Laurent costumes were arrayed according to visual schemes in daily or seasonal rhythms. The entryway evening-clothes gallery was devoted exclusively to variations on the theme of black and white. Thus outfits from different decades in Saint Laurent's development were disposed side by side, as testaments to the enduring primacy of black in evening wear as one essence of the designer's "genius." Along with color and time of day, the clothes were categorized by season—"fall/winter" ensembles, usually made of heavier fabrics, and "spring/summer" outfits of appropriately lighter weights. As in all the previous shows, guidance for the viewer was limited to labels full of mysterious fashion language delineating the stuffs of which the outfit was made ("silk gazar," "black jet," and the like). The net effect of the visual presentation was to emphasize a cyclical imperative in fashion: "Plus ça change, plus c'est la même chose." The visitor to the Saint Laurent exhibit was wafted into a boundless, fluid world united by an unbroken rhythm of seasons in which nights succeeded days and women continually changed their clothes.

The priority of surface over substance in the exhibit obscured, once again, important changes both internal and external to fashion that directly affected the designer. Vreeland praised YSL as a "Pied Piper" of fashion: "Where he goes, women of the world follow." In fact, exactly the opposite was true: Saint Laurent was a great adapter, and the many changes in his designs were like a sensitive barometer of changes in the values and expectations of his public. The most important element missing from Vreeland's visually anesthetizing exhibit was the political culture of the 1960s. Indeed, Saint Laurent was one of the first designers to respond to countercultural movements and to incorporate them into his fashions. In 1960 he inaugurated his "chic beatnik collection," which elevated black leather motorcycle jackets and black turtleneck sweaters into couture design. This collection was, according to the *New York Times*, a "disaster," causing an "uproar" in the fashion community: the young darling of international haute couture had succumbed to the "street's weirdo kooky influences." Later in the 1960s Saint Laurent turned again to the "street," this time the barricades. During the Paris student uprising of May 1968, he studied the appearance of those who manned the barricades. "He was struck," according to E. J. Dionne, Jr., in the *New York Times*, "by the way the men and women behind the barricades dressed—simply, in pants, shirts, and scarves." "They look beautiful because they are beautiful themselves," Saint Laurent said at the time. "They don't need anything else." The impact of the "beautiful" student radicals led him to simplify his couture and to develop an "army-navy" look. The combination of the barricade look and the women's movement also induced him to create a bold and new couture language—pants for women. Saint Laurent was among the first of the couturiers to respond in elite design to the emerging redefinition of male and female roles of the late sixties. He was credited with establishing a new norm in couture—the elegant, privileged, but comfortable and trousered woman, who adopted the simplicity of the counterculture while maintaining a respect for elite refinement.

Saint Laurent's genuine innovations in fashion, and his flirtation with the "street" and with the 1960s counterculture, were lost in the Vreeland show, melded into an undifferentiated and static image of an artist eternally dedicated to opulent femininity. Here once again Vreeland exercised her relentless practice of converting history into fantasy, complex reality into narcissistic image. The phases of Saint Laurent's own development as a designer, like the broader history of which it was a part, were reduced to titillating and predictable episodes of variations on black and white, to a procession of "fall/winter" to "spring/summer" collections. Vreeland blotted out from memory the profound challenge the sixties posed to the makers and wearers of couture; instead she projected a mesmerizing illusion of an uninterrupted cycle of spectacle and an unchanging elite dedicated to conspicuous consumption.

Saint Laurent himself collaborated in Vreeland's one-dimensional celebration of him. For just as Saint Laurent was a barometer of change rather than a leader, so he deftly adapted himself to the ethos of privilege regnant in Vreeland's Met. Saint Laurent actively participated in rewriting his own history for the show, and in promoting an illusion of an insulated elite world cultivating visible distinction. He used the retrospective as an occasion to publicly repudiate his youthful excesses of the sixties; he recanted his political dabblings and their democratizing fashion equivalents, and dedicated himself to the revival of elite haute couture. In a *New York Times* interview of December 4, 1983, he "issued a call to order." He criticized the sixties for its permissive *laisser aller*,—"too much letting go."

> There was too great a laisser-aller in fashion, which was even able to translate itself by a too great laisser-aller politically . . . a too great laisser-aller on the trademark of the country.

The *Times* reporter, Dionne, went on to characterize Saint Laurent as being engaged in a "counterrevolution," a new "conservatism" translated into a design based on "discipline," "order," and a return of French classicism.

Yet the lavish opulence of the Saint Laurent ensembles displayed in the Met show indicated that the designer's "new conservatism," like that of the Vreelandian elite who sponsored him, was hardly characterized by "discipline," "order," and classical restraint. Indeed, rather than a "counterrevolution" against the sixties, the Saint Laurent Met show celebrated the transvaluation of the values of the sixties: hedonism, license, self-indulgence, and permissiveness, charges once used to indict the youth culture of the sixties, were now transferred, via Vreeland, to the new Reaganite elite. The Met Saint Laurent boldly proclaimed that now it was the turn of the rich to enjoy the cult of irresponsibility hitherto reserved for and charged against sixties radicals.

Thus, despite the attempt to link couturier Saint Laurent and his illustrious clients with the aristocracies of the French past glorified in the other Vreeland shows, new meanings, peculiar to the 1980s, emerged to disassociate the past and present cult of privilege and conspicuous consumption. Press statements by Saint Laurent himself, and a part of the Vreeland exhibit, crystallized the themes underlying the aristocratic revival in 1983: decadence, narcissism, and sadism.

A large publicity campaign prepared the way for the opening of the Met Saint Laurent retrospective. Interviews with Saint Laurent appeared in *New York* magazine, the *New York Times*, *Vogue*, and *Time* magazine in early December. And a lavish catalogue on Yves Saint Laurent was produced for the Met, which included an essay by the designer. Significantly, in all of this literature, Saint Laurent presented himself to the public through a psychic unburdening; rather than describing the history and phases of his career, or explaining how his work was produced and commissioned, he engaged in a media confession. He spoke to the public as does a patient to a therapist, exposing the "anguish," "anxiety," and "suffering" that plagued him from his delicate youth to the height of his success. Narcissism transformed Saint Laurent from a producer of material objects into an aesthete dedicated to creating an image of his own ego as a work of art.

The press promoted Saint Laurent as a tormented "genius," as a sensitive "aesthete" racked by the relentless play of his imagination. *New York* magazine hailed Saint Laurent in its lead story, "All About Yves," as "a tall neurasthenic genius." In the three-page interview that followed, Saint Laurent recalled the "anguish" of his being "different, sensitive, and shy" as a child, which "traumatized me for life." He went on to reveal his constant "anxieties and fatigue," and his character as a "hypersensitive, reclusive neurotic." The *New York Times* repeated Saint Laurent's accounts of the "great traumatisms" of his "miserable childhood" and described his recollections of a "nervous collapse" suffered during his service in the French army. The December issue of *Vogue* devoted a long interview to Saint Laurent, who was presented as a "sensitive genius," a "dreamer," and an "aesthete," who "translated his memories and obsessions into his work." *Time* magazine similarly characterized Saint Laurent as a man who "radiates timidity and a fragile, overstrained sensibility," and delineated the number of times a week the designer visited his therapist and downed tranquilizers. The *Time* interviewer discussed with Saint Laurent his problem of being "incapable of loving or being loved." And the Met catalogue continued this psychic profile of Saint Laurent, publishing an essay by the designer about his anguished youth, nervous breakdown, and the psychic cost of his incessant creativity.

The Met's Saint Laurent evening coat

As Saint Laurent bared his psyche to the public, he also articulated his attraction to decadence and death. In both the Met catalog and *New York* magazine Saint Laurent proclaimed, "I love a dying frenzy. I love Visconti. Decadence attracts me. It suggests a new world, and for me, society's struggle between life and death is absolutely beautiful." In the *Vogue* interview Saint Laurent explained his use of black veils in couture as the "idea of death" and called his "idol" a "Black Virgin."

Yves Saint Laurent consciously associated his cult of decadence with the decadence fashionable in fin-de-siècle France. He adored Marcel Proust and expressed a deep identification with the late-nineteenth-century neurasthenic writer. In the Met catalogue and in *New York* magazine, Saint Laurent continually quoted Proust, and his description of the torments of his childhood and his memory of his mother's "good-night kiss" had a suspiciously Proustian tinge. Citing Proust, he claimed that he belonged, like the writer, to "the magnificent and pitiful family of the hypersensitive—it is they who have produced masterpieces." In this family of gifted, hypersensitive artists, Saint Laurent attached himself to Proust and his world, in which intellectual refinement compensated for physical frailty and timidity, but in which the psychic costs of creativity were neurosis and anxiety.

Following his role model, Saint Laurent noted that he perceived "mental suffering as a gift," a necessary spur to great art. His identification with Proust extended to a special architectural tribute. In a long photo essay in *Vogue* he revealed that he had built a château in Normandy to exact "Proustian specifications." The Château Gabriel comprised a series of rooms dedicated to the different characters from Proust's novels, each room decorated according to the precise tastes of that fictional character. A Guermantes room re-created a rococo suite at the Ritz, a favorite style and site of the duke and duchess. Saint Laurent inhabited a château room whose door was inscribed with the name Swann, the Proust character that he took as his alter ego. And Saint Laurent's partner and companion, Pierre Bergé, assumed the decor and role of the flamboyantly dominating Baron de Charlus. Here was an instance of life imitating art imitating life, an artifice twice removed, presented to *Vogue* readers as evidence of the cultivated and exquisite sensibility of Saint Laurent.

If fin-de-siècle decadence lent Saint Laurent an air of allure, his self-styled connection with Proust was as bizarre as Vreeland's. The publicity concentrated on Saint Laurent as a new Proust and as a hypersensitive aesthete promoted an illusion of a reclusive, private man living out his fantasies in a world apart. Yet this is the same man who runs and controls a business empire that rakes in two billion a year, and whose fantasies are continually funneled into the lucrative novelties sustaining the fashion market. Proust's own hypersensitivity and neurasthenic character made it impossible for him to negotiate the public world. Consigned to bed in a cork-lined room that shut out the street and market, he created novels of personal memory mediated by an exquisitely rendered social structure. Saint Laurent, on the other hand, was eminently capable of negotiating the public world. The promotion of his troubled aesthete image, like the lavish Proust tribute splashed across the pages of *Vogue,* offered the public a psychic gloss for a ruthlessly successful commercial genius.

Diana Vreeland installed the most extravagant and theatrical of Saint Laurent's costumes in the red room gallery, where YSL ensembles inspired by Chinese imperial robes appeared next to ornate variations on themes of Russian peasant clothes. Accompanying these exotic outfits were a series from Saint Laurent's "Spanish period." A spectator entering the red room was greeted on the right by a large gold-painted mannequin, draped in a massive cape that descended down the frame in avalanches of ruffles of bright "red and purple gazar." This was a Spanish-inspired "Picasso Evening Cape," lent by Diana Vreeland from her own Saint Laurent wardrobe. Across the room, on the spectator's left upon entering the red room, were two more Spanish figures. The first was a featureless lithe mannequin in a "Spanish Day Ensemble," consisting of "two pieces, with corselet bodice of black moiré and white cotton Bermuda shorts." Graced with a ruffle of red satin in her hair, this Spanish lady held her left arm on her hip and her right arm bent up to extend her long onyx cigarette holder. The second Spanish figure here was a gilded "toreador." Hands on hips, another thin, gold-painted mannequin displayed her "evening ensemble," three pieces, with toreador jacket and breeches of gold lamé brocade and black velvet, skirt of "Goya-green" moiré, and blouse of "black chiffon dotted with gold: shown with black velvet satin hat and black satin sandals."

This triptych of Spanish Saint Laurent ensembles was more than another restatement of the exhibit's opulent theme. For the mannequins were installed by Vreeland in relation to a peculiar backdrop, which added a startling sadistic twist to the gold and glitter of the Spanish evocations.

Vreeland, always searching for visual effects, borrowed Picasso paintings to complement the Saint Laurent Spanish fashions. Picasso was one of YSL's favorite painters, and elsewhere in the exhibit were displays of Saint Laurent's "Picasso dresses." Yet in the outlandish red room Vreeland posed the gilded and silken Spanish costumes in front of paintings from Picasso's "blue period," a period when he depicted ravaged figures from the Barcelona lower classes. At the entry to the right in the red room, the large faceless mannequin sheathed in the massive "Picasso Evening Cape" was set in front of a 1901 Picasso painting, *Girl Ironing*. The muted grays and flesh tones of the painting faded behind the bright red, gold, and purple of the lavish cape. The figure in the painting was limp and stooped over, her body contorted and her arms stretched by the unbroken cycle of moving the iron back and forth across a fabric. The figure in the painting was distinguishable only by her hair; her eyes were closed and her features hollowed out. The girl ironing was a faceless automaton, divested of her humanity by the strain of labor. Vreeland placed the fashion mannequin in Saint Laurent's "Picasso cape" in front of the painting in a strange position—the mannequin was turned so that her back faced the painting of the ironing girl, spreading out, like a peacock, the dazzling array of bright colored ruffles to confront the painting. Vreeland's placement of the other two Spanish mannequins was equally charged.

Across the room, the black corselet "Spanish day ensemble" figure and the gilded "evening toreador" flanked a large Picasso painting, the 1904 *Actor*. This actor was part of the underworld of street clowns and harlequins that Picasso repeatedly painted in this early phase. The large canvas depicted a standing harlequin, dressed in a mauve and pale blue costume. The figure was thin and haggard, with elongated face and neck and scrawny frame, evoking the meagerness of the street actor's world. The actor stared blankly off to the right, frozen in stillness and emptiness. His slim right arm was bent up in a strange curled hand gesture, showing very long fingers out-

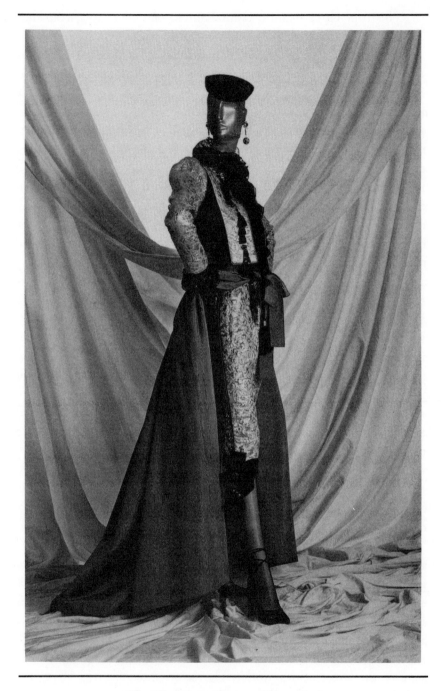

*The Met's Saint Laurent "Toreador"
ensemble of gold lamé and black velvet*

stretched. The bleakness of the scene in the painting contrasted sharply with the splendid gilded YSL mannequins poised in front of it. The Vreeland mannequins shared the elongated, slender frame of the actor; yet the Picasso figure was slim from hunger and emaciation while the Saint Laurent beauties were thin from the affluent thin look of self-denial or from anorexia nervosa. Vreeland's placement of the figures created a clear relationship between the mannequins and the painting. She pivoted both of the Spanish models so that they stood with the painting between them while they were turned with their faces toward the painting, looking directly into the picture plane. The mannequin in the Spanish black corselet and Bermuda shorts appeared on the left of the painting in a strange symmetry with the actor. The model's right hand extended, with the same elongated fingers curling as seen in the *Actor*. Yet at the tip of her fingers the YSL model held her cigarette holder while the actor's curled hand merely intensified the body's contorted elongation and haggard suffering. Vreeland's dazzling gold toreador model was positioned with her hands on hips at the right side of the Picasso painting, with her gold head and chin pointed up as she looked into the picture. She peered into the bleak Picasso underworld with a look of supreme detachment and contemptuous disdain.

Vreeland's intention in placing the YSL Spanish outfits with Picasso paintings as backdrops was probably conceived in purely visual terms: all the elements were formally Spanish, and the joining of the two artists, Picasso and YSL, provided interesting visual effects while elevating Saint Laurent's aesthetic status. Yet the ability to group the mannequins in relation to the paintings, without ever considering the subject of the paintings, typified Vreeland's amoral universe. Here at work was the Vreelandian roving eye, trained to look for surface images, visual shocks, detached from its subject and object—the same roving, amoral eye that had created the composite photos of dismembered body parts in *Vogue*. Beyond this testimony to Vreeland's epistemology, however, were broader social and political implications. The confrontations between the two sets of YSL mannequins with the Picasso paintings captured two elite attitudes binding Vreeland to Reaganite political culture. The first was exemplified by turning away, turning one's back on the poor. Vreeland posed her ruffle-caped mannequin with her magnificent back to the *Girl Ironing*, so that the

The Actor, *by Picasso*

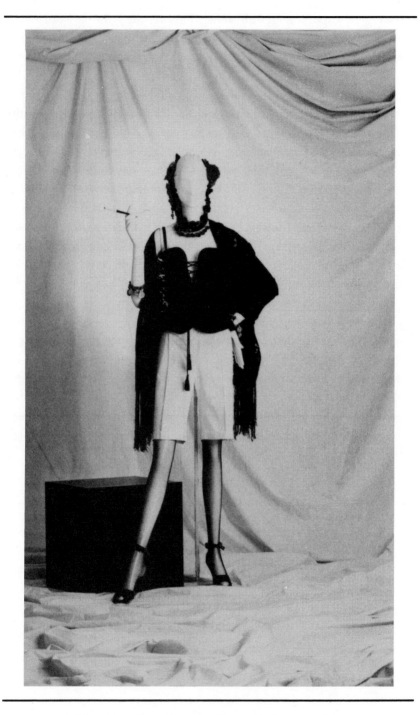

The Met's Saint Laurent "Spanish" day ensemble

extravagant cape was in full view. This recalled the byword of the Reaganites, "Living well is the best revenge," the reveling in insulated privilege while making emphatic and visible gestures of exclusion to everyone else: extravagant indulgence amidst great deprivation. The second attitude emerged in the confrontation between the two worlds. Vreeland's Spanish smoker and gold toreador stared into the painting of the hungry underworld of Picasso's actor with contempt, disdain, and supreme detachment. Here was an image redolent with Reagan's policies, which reached their culmination ten days after the opening of the Saint Laurent show. Insolence and cruelty surely characterized the attitude of then adviser to the president, Edwin Meese, toward the problem of the hungry in America, whose ranks have exploded as a result of Reagan's massive cutting of social programs. Meese claimed in December 1983 that evidence of hunger in America was merely "anecdotal" and that reports could not be "authenticated."

Meese's comments on the poor could have emanated from the icy lips of the YSL mannequins: "The allegations of hunger, of course, cannot be documented, and many who say they have nothing to eat really only want a free meal." In a moment when Scrooge was turned into a good employer (another of Meese's startling comments), and when the people on long soup-kitchen lines were depicted as cheaters and liars, the sadistic joining of gold fashion mannequins with paintings of the hungry poor in the museum assumed a particular, new, and more political meaning.

D.V., THE BESTSELLER

"SNIFFING OUT SOCIETY"

AND SELF-FASHIONING

1984

Your world . . . you have created it for
yourself, it is real to yourself, and therefore
real to us. . . . It is for you to discover yourself
in a world where, alone and free, you may
dream the possible dream: that the wondrous
is real, because that is how you feel it to be,
how you wish it to be . . . and how you wish
it into being.
———Diana Vreeland, *D.V.*, 1984

n the spring of 1984, while crowds continued to stream into the galleries of the Met Saint Laurent exhibition, Diana Vreeland launched her own personal retrospective: an autobiographical memoir entitled *D.V.* Published as a Borzoi book by Alfred E. Knopf, *D.V.* was a bestseller soon after it appeared. The volume's exclamatory dust-jacket touted it as "a pure pleasure to read," as an entrée into the world of "luxury among the century's chic, rich, and gifted," and as a portrait of the "dazzling life" of a "brilliant, funny, charming woman" endowed with a "passion and genius for style." The book was displayed, alongside the memorabilia of posters, scarves, catalogues, and postcards from the Saint Laurent exhibit, at the gift-shop station marking the entry and exit to the Costume Institute. Thus the retrospective of the "genius of haute couture" was bound to that of the *grande dame* who was his lifelong client and powerful promoter and who was now being celebrated as a genius in her own right.

The marketing of Vreeland's book in the Metropolitan Museum gift stalls elevated her status as curator-cum-illusionist to bizarre new heights. *D.V.* represented the culmination of Vreeland's career with the Met, an association that had evolved from an uneasy embarrassment into a vaunted institution. Vreeland recounted in her memoir how she had been enlisted by her friend Ted Rousseau, an official of the Met, to work with the museum's costume collection, and how Rousseau "installed" her in an office in 1972. At the time, museum staff members saw her arrival as a spur to public visibility for the costume section, which had been closed for renovations for four years. Writer Jesse Kornbluth investigated the initial arrangements between the Met and Mrs. Vreeland and characterized them as tense and ambiguous. The original plan was for a group of Vreeland's wealthy friends to donate $1,000 each to pay her salary. When the money failed to materialize, museum officials resisted, but eventually hired Vreeland onto the staff as consultant-curator. In the early stages of debate, some at the Met expressed their dissatisfaction with granting Mrs. Vreeland an official position in the museum; one former administrator told Kornbluth that Vreeland "knows fashion and who wore it but she doesn't know *history*."

Vreeland's activities in her first year at the Met realized the reluctant officials' worst expectations. Traveling worldwide to collect costumes for special exhibitions and collections, she spared no expense, and presented her accounts for payment by the museum's treasury. The luxurious Hotel Crillon was the only place in Paris where she would stay; she also would not travel without hiring a personal limousine and chauffeur. Her colleagues at the Costume Institute were equally offended at her erratic and unprofessional behavior. Kornbluth interviewed museum assistants who recalled how Vreeland would alter the plan and contents of exhibitions without warning, after consulting with "famous people"—fashion designers and socialites—whose advice she favored over that of hard-working staff members. Assistants soon learned to counterattack by sneaking their own work back into the galleries the night before the exhibition openings.

Diana Vreeland's integration into the Met as an indispensable figure followed the Hoving program for the mass expansion and commercialization of the museum. Her abrasive and unscholarly postures fit into the museum's search for unconventional and crowd-pleasing techniques to attract new people and new money. By 1980, Vreeland had triumphed over her critics and co-workers on the museum staff and had become one of the Met's greatest assets: her exaggerated personal style captured media attention, while her social connections were tapped for funds. She had turned the Costume Institute's exhibition gala openings into a major event on the New York elite social calendar. The December 7 party was oversubscribed, and invitations to it were coveted as a high point of the winter social season.

Vreeland's memoir, *D.V.*, concentrated, in the form of personal history, the contradictory themes so central to her museum oeuvre: the idolization of aristocratic distinction and luxury; the rootless and ruthless self-creation that simulated a style of aristocratic stability; and the aggressive substitution of fantasy for reality, the dissolution of fact by wish. Vreeland's autobiographical memoir illuminates the personality and value system that generated the peculiar configuration of the costume shows, and points to their origins in her personal history and fantasy.

The formal structure of *D.V.* adheres to the antichronological principle of organization that marked Vreeland's museum presentations. *D.V.* is a memoir without memory, an autobiography without time. The text consists of thirty-two short, choppy, numbered sections transcribed from taped conversations with George Plimpton and Christopher Hemphill. The sections unfold in random succession, unconnected to each other and lacking the textual markers of the phases of life history that usually give a narrative of this kind a shape of beginnings, middles, and ends. For a woman who states "I hate old people," assuming the conventional voice of age looking back is anathema; and her uninterrupted decades devoted to "artifice, dressing, and making up" render a textured retelling of personal history impossible. Instead, the memoir collapses a jumble of tidbits of family history; parades the names, origins, and adventures of European aristocrats and royalty, Indian princes, Argentinian polo players, and American upper-crust "swells" with whom Vreeland ostensibly socialized; and bursts with Vreeland's startling aphorisms concerning color, food, women, shoes, race, and the decline of the West.

Vreeland's *D.V.* voice darts in and out of time, events, and advice in a way that resembles the pace, shock, and constantly changing focus she cultivated, to great success, in the pages of *Vogue*. The jarring, unordered form of the text may be compelling to former *Vogue* readers familiar with Vreeland's photo collages or her plan to publish *Vogue* in reverse sequence, "pretending it was a Japanese book." Despite its disordered and rambling shape, *D.V.* has been prepared with respectful and elegant care by Knopf. The sleek, smoothly finished black book jacket is emblazoned with a painted color portrait of Mme. Vreeland, a full-length seated view typical of traditional European royal portraiture. Her expansive chair-throne is raised from the floor on a stone pedestal, and the two stately columns framing it echo the fine, chiseled ivory features of the figure's face. This composed image on the book cover contrasts sharply with the restless, jagged, and inchoate text within.

The "pleasure" of reading promised by the book's blurb is broken by the very first sentence on the first page: "I loathe nostalgia." The opening statement of hate is immediately followed by acts of aggression: Vreeland recounts how she punched Swifty Lazar, a literary agent, in the nose and then the chest, shattering a china platter he had placed there to protect his heart from Vreeland's fists, because he had accused her of reveling in nostalgia. This strange introductory episode—Vreeland violently rejecting nostalgia—launches a book that is openly calculated to appeal to snobbish nostalgia, emanating from a woman whose celebrity status derives from her capacity to invoke lost worlds of luxury and privilege. At the same time, the graphic smashing of nostalgia also appropriately sets the tone for the book, which celebrates the destruction of time and memory. Nostalgia presupposes the differentiation of a prior historical world from an experienced present condition. Vreeland's *D.V.* motto, "FAKE IT, FAKE IT," banishes nostalgia for fabrication; in a world where reality is what "you wish it to be, as you wish it into being," nostalgia dissolves amidst successive moments of vigorous self-invention.

The contents of *D.V.* offer compelling parallels between Vreeland's life and her museum practice and establish the themes of the Met shows in her personal history. Vreeland appears in *D.V.* as a living mannequin who experiences the world as a series of endless, extravagant fabrications. Her cult of artifice and making up leads her to mold herself, variously, in the guises of Chinese empress, rococo aristocrat, Belle Epoque demimondaine and Saint Laurent gilded toreador.

One theme of Vreeland's autobiography celebrates indolence, leisure, and the life of perpetual pleasure that Vreeland attributes in her shows to privileged elites. Vreeland describes her early life, first with her parents in Paris and New York, and then as Reed Vreeland's wife, as being completely free of work. Her parents, who became "racy, pleasure-loving Parisians," spent their days "having a good time—they never contributed anything, and they and their friends lived the life of Riley." Her father, a Scottish stockbroker, disappeared frequently for weeks at a time, while "he never made any money and never thought about money." Vreeland's mother, a "flamboyant" American, "was one of the beauties of La Belle Epoque in Paris," "living only for excitement," and proceeding, according to *D.V.*, from one scandalous love affair to the next. Surrounded by servants and chauffeurs, and present at endless evening parties, young Diana was taught to curtsy and to plant good-night kisses on the cheeks of such of her parent's guests as Diaghilev, Lord Guinness, and handsome Turkish "charmers" temporarily infatuated with her mother.

When the family moved to New York in 1914, Diana, unlike other children, was liberated from the tedium of formal education and did as she wished. After a brief stint at Brearley, she studied dancing with Fokine and patterned herself after her mother. Living "only for excitement" and "always making a show," she dedicated herself to "getting ready to go out in the evening." She engaged in protracted competition with her mother, who repeatedly provoked the daughter's wrath by insisting on flirting with her boyfriends. It was difficult for Vreeland to outdo the mother in matters of appearance and flamboyant presentation; Mrs. Dalziel was not only naturally beautiful but used layers of makeup so as to appear as if she were totally painted. Diana, whom her mother nicknamed "my ugly little monster," transposed her natural disadvantage by playing her mother's tricks to the extreme: she literally painted the upper half of her body white, after "discovering calcimine." "Calcimined from the waist up," socialite D.V. danced the tango through the nights, taking great pleasure in the effect of heightened contrast with her red lacquered fingernails and her escorts' black dinner jackets. The appearance of spray-painted gold mannequins in the Met exhibitions, their glistening bony frames sharply offsetting their clothes, extends the extreme strategy of self-fashioning Vreeland had practiced on her own body. As in the allure she ascribed to Belle Epoque beauties, Vreeland shaped her own persona as a total work of artifice, designed, as she reiterated in her shows, "to overwhelm and silence her rivals."

Vreeland's marriage in 1924 to Reed Vreeland, a Yale graduate in training as a banker, took her to Albany and London, where she continued her devotion to clothes, entertaining, and never dressing until it was time for lunch. Her household, run by servants and house-maids, freed her to have "nothing to do." For a short time, while they lived in London, Mrs. Vreeland ran a lingerie store, commissioning made-to-order lace and satin bed sheets, nightgowns, and under-garments. Among the clients who could afford the luxurious hand-made work and prices was Wallis Simpson, soon to become the Duchess of Windsor.

Reed Vreeland shared his wife's love of luxury and travel. De-scribing him as a "quiet, elegant, beautiful" man, D.V. admired Reed's care with dressing and recounts how he had their butler "polish his shoes for five years or so with cream and rhinoceros horn until they were the *essence* of really contented leather—only then did he wear them." Emphasizing that they *never* spoke about business, and that she knew as little about Reed's banking activities as of her own father's mysterious profession, Vreeland portrays her life with Reed as a whirlwind of luxurious, "divine," and seemingly permanent vacations. Tunisia, Bavaria, Budapest, Capri, Antibes—the Vreelands "made a point of going to out-of-the-way new places" rather than to "chic *villes d'eau*" like their predictable and unimaginative con-temporaries. D.V. recounts how the couple, leaving their two sons in the care of the house staff and two nannies, "only went where the air was fragrant and life was easy," motoring about in their "glorious Bugatti," accompanied by their housemaid and chauffeur. At each destination the Vreelands were greeted by illustrious hosts and extra-ordinary sensual delights. One of the many hosts was the Baron d'Erlanger, who welcomed the Vreelands to his Tunisian palace on the Mediterranean. As they were escorted to their quarters by a score of menservants, their path was cleared by a dazzling herd of rare white peacocks. "Our life," sighs Vreeland, "was a dream of beauty."

The "strenuous" parts of the Vreelands' European travels were Diana's fittings in Paris. Mme. Vreeland was very "involved with clothes," and she was in the habit of being fitted for all of her outfits, including nightgowns, which usually called for three fittings. Hats, gloves, and shoes were also custom-made, composing "a whole life." "The life of fashion," notes Vreeland, "was very strenuous." Interestingly, Vreeland explains that she was often treated by the couture houses to a special price—nothing—for her outfits. Her self-defined role as a traveling socialite and fashion plate rendered her a *mannequin du monde*," a living model, whom the couturiers subsidized in return for chic visibility. In between these twice-yearly "pilgrimages" for fittings in Paris, Vreeland's maid, Yvonne, would "meticulously stain and polish all shoes after each wearing—including the soles."

Vreeland's representation of her own life as an uninterrupted spectacle of beauty, "luxury, perfume, flowers," and the exquisite relishing of "every day as totally and completely new," corresponded to her museum projections of historical elites endlessly enjoying high living in blissful obliviousness to social, political, and cultural change. Like that of her eighteenth-century women, Vreeland's world was "marked by extravagance and splendor," in which "light, opportunity and exultation were everywhere." Like the mood of Belle Epoque "hi livers," Vreeland's mood was always "buoyant, ebullient, and delicious," and she was always surrounded by "laughter, fun, lots of romance, and *great* style." The D.V. in Vreeland's book, like the mannequins inhabiting her imagined historical worlds, lived in an untextured zone, divested of pain, constrained only by the perpetual daily rhythm of changing her clothes.

Yet Vreeland's exhibition of her own past as a perfect living dream recklessly denies discordant elements of personal and social reality, and is marked by the same aggressive will to fantasy that shaped her museum shows. The leveling of experience into undifferentiated moments of sensory stimulation and delectation misrepresents Vreeland's own past as much as those of the disparate historical elites she eagerly claimed lived a life so similar to our own. Just as she had transformed the eighteenth century into a "century of revolution in fashion," the Belle Epoque into an era of "delicious hypocrisy and innocent naughtiness," and Yves Saint Laurent into a lofty new Picasso, so Vreeland depicts the 1930s and 1940s as a time when "the air was fragrant and life was easy," when "life was a dream of beauty." In passing sections of *D.V.*, as in occasional pockets of the Met exhibitions, the complex, conflictual, and painful character of historical realities pops out of the sensory-surface frame. Vreeland's allusions to contextual material, particularly the European events of the 1930s and 1940s, reveals a distanced, trivializing posture designed to shock, grab, and create novel effects. Only supreme detachment and amorality could allow Vreeland to revel as she does in reminiscences of violent episodes, turning them into comic and titillating events.

We will not dwell here on the scope and origins of personal feelings of pain, shame, abandonment, and envy that Vreeland hints in *D.V.* fueled her relationship to her mother. Vreeland invokes her father's example of quoting the telltale aphorism "Worse things happen at sea" in any and all family crises. She records, and then glosses quickly over, how she painted herself white from the waist up to elicit some response from her remote and absent parents. She also skirts the personal wound she suffered when one of her mother's many amorous affairs was publicized in the newspapers in the days preceding her wedding, and when none of the invited guests appeared at the wedding ceremony, as her mother had forgotten to mail the invitations. In bracing strides of denial, Vreeland proclaims, "Never mind—bash on—never look back!"

Personal pain is largely contained in *D.V.*; more prominent is Vreeland's projection of aggression and unbearable feelings outward, revealing a fascination with violence, murder, and sadism. And the denial of personal anguish is paralleled by a denial of historical and social crisis, which leads her to sardonic and insolent comments on periods of war, deprivation, and unspeakable human suffering.

The episode of shattering fists with which *D.V.* opens is echoed throughout in the peculiar bantering tone of the book. Vreeland recounts how she witnessed two murders during her youth. Owing to a polio scare, her mother had sent her and her sister off to Wyoming, where, claims D.V., the girls rode horses and befriended Colonel Cody—Buffalo Bill. One night the children witnessed a shoot-out in the street below their hotel. As men fell dead, D.V. notes that she wasn't frightened; she considered the episode "totally bizarre—it didn't affect us that much." Later, on a late-night jaunt in a New York nightclub, Vreeland and her friends were escorted out by police—

a gang shoot-out had occurred on the entry steps to the club. Vreeland recalls how she walked over three men slumped on the stairs, "bleeding to death." Her next sentence, her supposed reminiscence of her reaction to the horrible scene, consists of her remembering exactly what she wore—"white satin dress and white satin slippers"—and the contrasting color effect created by the red blood that spattered on her white satin slippers.

Vreeland's youthful contact with violent death led her, as she claims in *D.V.*, to cultivate a certain attitude in her own children: 'I made a solemn vow never to allow my children to know that anything in the world was frightening, impure, or impossible." D.V. had herself learned "not to be afraid of anything physical or strange or bizarre," like murder, and she wanted her sons to know that same sense of sangfroid and assurance. Vreeland notes that on their nanny's day off, she would take her boys to "Madame Tussaud's Wax Museum and see the beheadings." She continues:

> That was a bit of all right for them. Nothing wrong for them to see. Everybody had to go! All I can say is that my sons had a very healthy upbringing. And they've gone through life the same way. They've never been afraid of anything . . . physical or strange or bizarre.

Vreeland then moves from provocative object lessons for her sons to the events of the 1930s. In one passage frequently quoted by reviewers as the essence of Vreelandian pluck and unpredictability, she explains how she was in Paris for her yearly fittings at Chanel when the war broke out, and that her husband gallantly left her to complete her ensembles of skirts of "silver lamé" and "lace bolero encrusted with pearls and diamanté," and to order her pairs of handmade shoes. She then laments how depressed she was as she prepared to board the "last passenger ship with private cabins out of Europe," for she would have to leave her beloved couture behind. Vreeland returned to Paris right after the war, eager to renew her fittings. On remembering her postwar arrival, her comments were that the quality of French bread had declined sharply owing to the use of potato flour and that couture had also undergone two devastating changes: the *"prix jeune fille"* ($0) offered to Vreeland as a *"mannequin du monde"* had been eliminated, along with fittings for nightgowns. Such were Vreeland's reactions to Europe in the immediate aftermath of World War II.

Vreeland turns her attention in another section to Hitler and the Nazis and claims she was in the hotel when the Röhm massacre occurred. Typically, she transforms this significant historical event into another outrageous bit of trivial personal chitchat, which she uses to distinguish her astonishing range of "novel" experiences and to inflate her own celebrity. Whether she really was there on the "night of the long knives" or not is less important than the attitude she brings to her materials. We find, then, in chapter 11 of *D.V.* Vreeland recounting how on one of her 1934 motor trips through Bavaria with Reed, she stayed at the classy Munich Vier Jahreszeiten Hotel. As always, the Vreelands' every moment was packed with luxury and delight: they spent their days in Swan Country "having picnics and revisiting the castles of mad King Ludwig, which we could never see enough of." After wandering through Nymphenberg, Neuschwanstein, Linderhof, and Herrenchiemsee by day, the couple returned to their hotel for dinner and concerts. One evening they made their way back to the hotel to find a commotion at the entry and huge Mercedes-Benzes blocking the façade. Near the cars appeared Röhm and his Nazi officers, and a regiment of "goose-stepping soldiers" saluted them, "Heil! Heil! Heil!" D.V. was very annoyed by all this to-do—she was "in a hurry to change her clothes and get to a concert." She pushed her way through the officers, shouting, "Excuse me, excuse me, I've got to get to my bath!" Reed was mortified and entreated his wife to "behave yourself—you are in someone else's country and it's been taken over by this special breed of people." Once she had made it to her bath and concert, Vreeland gave no more thought to the noisy "captains of Hitler's new order." She expressed her annoyance with them on aesthetic grounds: Röhm and his officers had no taste—they lumbered about in "overcoats to the ground, with spiked helmets, swords jangling, and spurs," making grating "metallic" sounds and appearing so clumsy. Vreeland resented the Nazi officers on two counts: Their outfits and bearing provided an unwanted lowbrow "contrast" of "absurd, comic-opera bullies" with her own elegant, nuanced world of sensual perfection, and they dared to delay her bath and dressing! Vreeland's personal maid, Julie, complained in the following days that "something terrible was happening" in the suites of the German officers, but D.V. scolded her, telling her to mind her own business: as long as one could get from one's room to where one wanted to go, it was of no concern. Vreeland claims she later understood how her savvy maid was trying to inform her of the Röhm murders in the hotel.

To conclude her reminiscence of the "Nazis I have known" sequence, Vreeland turns from the "comic-opera bullies" of Germany to pornography in France. She revels in explaining that Visconti's depiction of the Röhm officers in women's underwear was true—she had seen photographs of German officers who occupied her friend Elsie Mendl's property at Versailles "running around in Elsie's underclothes." Elsie's caretaker had snapped the photos and, Vreeland emphasizes, "They were *some* pictures!"

Vreeland's focus on Nazis and kinky sexuality provides a key to a central theme of *D.V.*: the leveling of social distinctions through sexual desire, and women's unique ability to cross social boundaries by using their sexual power. Beneath the idolization of aristocratic lineage and etiquette pervading Vreeland's memoirs—as well as her museum exhibits—is a wicked propensity to expose the seamy side of the titled nobility. Similarly, Vreeland delights in detailing the upward mobility of lower-class females through sex.

D.V. offers evocations of the splendid coronation of George V and of Vreeland's supposedly equally splendid presentation at the London court of the king and his wife, Queen Mary. Yet Vreeland introduces her stories of the propriety and luxury of royalty by an anecdote about the techniques of Queen Mary's masseur and describes the queen being massaged in the nude. This voyeuristic trivialization continues in most cases where Vreeland invokes an aristocratic or royal personality. Lord Guinness, we are told early on in the book, exemplified a particularly English strategy for upper-class gentlemen— that of publicizing their liaisons with female courtesans while they were really only using the women "as a front" for their sexual activities with "the boys." A sponsor of Diaghilev's Ballets Russes, Lord Guinness "was one of the great keepers of Paris women," according to *D.V.*, "protecting his reputation" while privately exercising his preference behind the doors of the demimonde. Intimate attention is also lavished on women who entered the nobility "through the back door."

As *vendeuse* in her luxury lingerie boutique, Vreeland was able to find out when Mrs. Simpson planned her first overnight assignation with the Prince of Wales, and the reader is regaled with the prices and varieties of satin, lace, and silk nightgowns ordered for the occasion. Elsewhere we learn that Rosa Lewis, proprietess of the Cavendish Hotel in London, was the "mistress of Edward VII and was passed on to Lord Ribbesdale," who then left her the hotel. Vreeland reserves special mention for two women of "low" origins and their spectacular rise: Marion Davies, "an alive, electric creature of total charm . . . and power," who "had sold oranges in the street and now she slept with a king"—William Randolph Hearst; and Coco Chanel, "a peasant," who learned everything she knew about luxury from two illustrious men in her life—the Duke of Westminster, who taught her horsemanship and the elegance of afternoon teas in country estates, and Grand Duke Dmitri of Russia, who showed her "great Romanov jewels and great living."

Vreeland's fascination with the demimonde provided an organizing principle for her Met presentation of the eighteenth-century woman and the 1890s Belle Epoque. *D.V.* registers the centrality of the demimonde in Vreeland's own past and personal fantasies. Pages of the book are devoted to rapturous comments on the glamour, extravagance, and exquisite pleasures of the world where the elite and most expensive European courtesans mingled with the highest strata of European male society. Vreeland notes, in chapter 2, that "my dreams are in the Bois," where the "*cocottes*," "the great personalities of Paris" paraded early to take the morning air and to exhibit their "extraordinary beauty" and "glamorous dress." The women were a tribute to their sex, and "to the men who kept them." Later on in *D.V.* the demimonde reappears, at a villa in Cannes owned by a "charming, well-born" Argentinian, Dodero, "one of Perón's henchmen." At Dodero's soirée Vreeland encountered many demimondaines, mingling with Aly Khan, the Marquis de Portago, and Rita Hayworth. She imagined the party as resembling the Proust sections she had just reread, which, as only she remembered it (wrongly), featured a "demimondaine turning up at a party for the Duchesse de Guermantes." At one point Vreeland, who had always carried red camellias, though these were disparaged by her mother as the flowers that cocottes carried when they were "unavailable," decided to see a modern equivalent of the demimonde world she dreamt of from her Parisian youth. Sometime in the 1930s, as she and Reed embarked on another of their interminable pleasure trips, they spent the night in Marseilles and arranged for a "tour of the red-light district." Vreeland describes the tour as an "evening prowl" into the underworld, where they eagerly proceeded, despite their guide's warnings of danger and violence. Vreeland was thrilled—the brothel they visited was called Edward VII, linking her own voyeurism with her interest in the libertine adventures of European royalty. She and Reed found the scene "extraordinary." Musicians played; they saw rooms of mirrors, silver, and gold, and that evening's lineup of female offerings. While recalling that she and Reed lived for the moment, for everything new and different, she notes that they found the Marseilles experience "attractive" and "extraordinary"—the brothel was "where earth and sky meet."

Earth and sky—the extremes of aristocratic reserve and demimondaine extroversion—are indeed two sides of Vreeland herself. The jacket of her book visually captures the two extremes. In the front of the book we behold the stately enthroned portrait, with sea and sky in the distance, followed by images of Vreeland's elegant, discreet femininity on the inside pages. As we move to the back of the book, we find D.V. the female vamp and demimondaine—in bright red gilded dressing gown with bright red nails and ruby lips, poised emphatically on a bright red sofa enveloped by busy, glaring red drapery and papered walls. Earth and sky meet, too, in *D.V.*

Vreeland's youthful apprenticeship—her total involvement with clothes and self-fabrication; her access to illustrious social circles and to aristocracies of heritage and money; her dedication to perpetual stimulation and to novelty, whenever it could be cultivated; and her fascination with female conquests through aesthetic seduction and sexual power—these formative attitudes became the ingredients of Vreeland's personal success. After moving to New York with her family in 1937, she found that her husband's income did not stretch as far as it had in Europe, and she "was going through money like one goes through . . . a bottle of scotch, if you're an alcoholic." The editor of *Harper's Bazaar*, who had seen D.V. dancing at the St. Regis, asked her to join the magazine—she liked Vreeland's style: on that night the living mannequin wore a white-lace Chanel dress, bolero, and red roses in her hair. Vreeland, nonplussed, responded that with the exception of her lingerie shop, she had never worked a day in her life, and *never* dressed till lunch, but since she had "dedicated hours and hours of detailed time to clothes," and knew where to have them made, she might be suited for the job. "Suddenly," exclaims Vreeland, "I found that my whole background was my future."

Vreeland achieved success as a fashion editor by marketing her fantasies of luxury, snobbism, and self-creation through changing visual appearance. She carried her social connections and her provocations into a variety of editorial projects. Her fascination with the world of elite European courtesans led her to publish a "little black book," given to *Harper's* by a *"chasseur"* at Maxim's, listing all the demimondaines of the Belle Epoque. The book described each woman and her distinguishing attractions and special defects. *Harper's* readers were thus treated to minutiae concerning women for sale: which courtesan had a "mole on her left hip," which was kept by this or that baron, and which had had her value raised by her liaison with a certain duke. Vreeland also brought notoriety to her magazine by her discovery of the "thonged sandal," an open shoe with a single strap between the first two toes. Vreeland claims to have been inspired to copy the sandal from the pornographic museum at Pompeii, to which she gained access in the 1940s "through a friend in the Mussolini government." The Pompeii museum contains wall paintings that capture the horror and frenzy of human activities in the "minute and a half after a volcanic eruption." Amidst the cataclysm of writhing, suffering bodies, Vreeland's eye was riveted to an image of her favorite theme: sex between beautiful people from opposite ends of the social scale. She describes in *D.V.* "a woman having an affair with her slave," and the slave was wearing the sandals fated to be revived by *D.V.* for stylish American women readers of *Harper's Bazaar*. Having had a pair of the sandals copied for her own use, Vreeland was delighted to be strutting about in the footwear of Roman slaves of yore.

Despite her assertions of female dependency and male superiority in parts of *D.V.*, Vreeland celebrates a rigorous ethic of female power and of the cultivation of a ruthless, imperial self. She invokes three women in her book as her models—women who used men and who "ruled empires" by their unbending will and driving ambition. One, Diane de Poitiers, was the companion of a king, whom Vreeland

glorifies for her "fantastic discipline" and the "motto over her bed—
Seule." Unflinching control was also the quality of two contemporary
businesswomen of fashion, Helena Rubinstein and Coco Chanel—
rivals and strong personalities. Vreeland admires the way they molded
themselves as works of art and carried that artifice into the market:

> They both came from nothing. They both were so much richer
> than most of the men we talk about today being rich. They'd
> done it all alone. Of course, there'd been men in their lives . . .
> but they earned every cent they made. . . . They were in
> power, at the wheel . . . running everything . . . these two
> women ruled empires.

Ruling alone and being the power at the wheel were Vreeland's own
values in asserting her imperious authority in her editorial work. She
developed a motto as she invented extreme fashion novelties for the
monthly magazine; it involved her disdain for facts. "Never worry
about facts," she said; "project an image to the public." The business
of fashion demanded the public exercising of the ethic of personal
self-fabrication that Vreeland had defined from her youth. She exhorts
us to pretend, to "fake it," to work only for "*results,*" and find the
way to those results by any means possible.

The world of aristocratic idealization projected by *D.V.* is finally
shattered from within—a casualty of the sexual, commercial, and
individual amorality that lies at its core. This world, "as you wish
it to be, as you wish it into being," is memorialized not only in a
best-selling publication but in works of museum "education."

As Vreeland's position in the Met has solidified as museum policy
shifted, so too her presence outside the museum has expanded with
the antiethics of the 1980s. In her earlier incarnation as fashion editor,
she had been subjected to stark satire, from Sylvia Plath's book *The
Bell Jar* to the film *Funny Face.* In her new prominence as museum
curator and social hobnobber, Diana Vreeland is not only tolerated
but celebrated, and her autobiography has been greeted with un-
critical acclaim. The exaggerated anecdotes and outrageous remarks
in *D.V.*, covering everything from the animalic bodies of blacks to the
natural mental inferiority of women, articulate in caricature, in extreme form, ideas and feelings that subsisted but were considered in-

admissible in past years. Vreeland's distorted humor and stance allow the reader to snicker, joke, and mock things in a way that hitherto was regarded as impermissible but is now being invested with new respectability. The glorification of Diana Vreeland as curator and as autobiographer suggests that she has come to occupy a space in the public imagination vacated by social concern and compassionate self-extension.

"SPIT AND POLISH AND GREAT TAILORING"

MAN, THE HORSE, AND
RALPH LAUREN'S POLO
AT THE MET
1984–1985

There is a way of living that has a certain grace and beauty. It is not a constant race for what is next, rather, an appreciation of what has come before. There is a depth and quality of experience that is lived and felt, a recognition of what is truly meaningful. . . . This is the quality of life that I believe in. . . . There is a romance of living, a beauty in things that endure. . . .
—Ralph Lauren, Polo ads, 1984

During the months of preparation for Ronald Reagan's second presidential inauguration, the Metropolitan Museum opened its newest Vreelandian creation: the Costume Institute's tribute to "Man and the Horse." The generic title belied a very specific and exclusive interpretation of equestrian history. "Man and the Horse" filled the museum's galleries with the riding habits, accessories, boots, bridles, saddles, trunks, whips, carriages, and polo mallets used in the most elite and most traditional of sports: the hunt, the polo match, and the private horse race. The exhibition, which opened on December 18, 1984, had nothing whatever to do with the costumes and accoutrements of transportation, with agriculture, or with the functional pairing of men and their beasts of burden or speed. From the poster for the show depicting a seated English lord in his riding habit being attended by servants in his country estate to the catalogue inscribed on its front jacket with the statement: "A prince is never surrounded by as much majesty on his throne as he is on a beautiful horse," the Met embraced Diana Vreeland's voyeuristic remaking of history into episodes of aristocratic leisure. Declaring that "the association of man and his horse" is "all elegance and cleanliness, lean and shine, spit and polish, tweeds and the open air," Vreeland glorified the horse as the "most sensitive piece of living beauty," as the essence of "breeding" and "gleaming, regal movements." Vreeland's exhibition thus focused on those human companions whose pedigree, precision, and attention to sartorial quality were worthy of

The cover of the Met catalogue for the
"Man and the Horse" show, 1984

what she called the "splendor" and "esprit" of "this remarkable animal."

In introducing the show, Philippe de Montebello emphasized that the exhibition commemorated "the splendor of equestrian attire," which "reflected man's desire to emulate the nobility of the horse." One theme of the exhibition, noted the museum director, was the "timeless quality and superior design" generated for the world of elite equestrian play and the continuity of style, social status, and tradition that the "horsey set" represented. De Montebello also pointed to the extreme refinement of tailoring and craftsmanship articulated in the riding uniform and equestrian implements, which lifted the show out of the realm of "merely fashionable effects" to the "essence of true style." Both Vreeland and de Montebello contrasted the novelty and transience of fashion to the durability and continuity of the rituals of exclusive horsemanship and horse ownership. In that world of the horse, these museum organizers assured, both costume and etiquette had been nurtured, largely unchanged, since the eighteenth century.

The contrasts between style and fashion, between enduring beauty and transient effect, between timeless quality and fleeting novelty, between depth of tradition and rootless competition—these were also concerns expressed by designer Ralph Lauren. Vreeland and de Montebello explicated the appeal of the Met history of equestrian costume as having to do with its embodiment of style, tradition, and quality. Ralph Lauren evoked an English well-born horsey style in his Polo fashions, what he described as "an old money look." Initially successful for promoting sportswear centered on the American denim jean, Lauren upgraded his designs, focusing on the Anglophile sportsman of the polo shirt. Lauren's signature, Polo, was associated with what he called a "sport that had an aristocratic image." The logo comprises a mounted polo player with a raised mallet, depicted in recent advertisements in huge close-up frames and bearing a striking resemblance to Prince Charles at his favorite sport.

Since 1983 Lauren has extended his fashion empire into "complete life-style marketing"—interior design and home-furnishing items, from bed linens to bathroom accessories. Organized in themes, one of the first home-furnishing Polo lines was called "Thoroughbred." Photographed in lavish advertisements, "Thoroughbred" encompassed one-

MONSIEVR, ROY DE PERSE.

The frontispiece for the catalogue for "Man and the Horse"

hundred-percent cotton paisley sheets and a wool challis throw to enable the buyer to inhabit the simulated world of horse owners or riders. The ads contained background objects such as polished wood and leather trunks for polo implements and riding gear, suggesting the appropriate completion of the "Thoroughbred" ensemble. In the fall of 1984 Lauren unfolded a tribute to the English gentry, splayed in photo suites of advertisements across the pages of major magazines. A series of ten full-page color ads for Polo began with a boldly printed statement by Ralph Lauren, which was adjacent to a photo of the entry to a stately country house. Lauren's comments, quoted above, glorified the "way of living" endowed with "beauty and grace," which is anchored in "what has come before" rather than the "race for what is next." The "way of living" thus suggested was made visible in the weather-beaten stone columns and portico of the manor, and in the old, black, basketed bicycle leaning comfortably on the stone piers. The nine remaining pages of the Polo ads enhanced the aura and appeal of gracious, traditional gentry living. The full view of the estate and its acres of lawn was provided on the third page, complemented by photos of women and children in Polo fashions reclining on the grounds. The photos taken inside the mansion featured individual figures or groups framed by family heirlooms or ancestral portraits. The fifth page, for example, displayed a discreet woman in a blue suit with a group of three children; in back of them was a piano brimming with family photos, and in the distance loomed a large painted portrait of another mother with her brood. Pages 7 and 10 evoked the world of elite equestrian sport, offering images of knee-high riding boots, books with stags on their covers, and piano photos of mounted polo players and riders. The last page of the Polo ensemble confronted the viewer with two white pedigreed dogs lounging in the living room and looking directly outward. Beneath them Lauren's words again exhorted: "There is a romance to living, a beauty in things that endure and have personal meaning."

Lauren beckoned his readers to inhabit the world associated with Polo, to step into a fabric of beauty comprised in permanent, meaningful things. The magic of the Polo logo would bring to the buyer the aura of "beauty in things that endure," though these things might rapidly be replaced and reprocessed for the newest line of fashion. The beauty in things that "have personal meaning" would be instantly provided by the Polo/Lauren label, which would nourish its multitude of possessors with the illusion of distinction, quality, and the "personal" signature.

Ralph Lauren's glorification of landed English gentry—their horses, polo matches, and ancestral continuity—struck a resonant chord among the planners of the Metropolitan Museum's Costume Institute exhibition for 1984. Lauren's shift from the image of frontiersman to polo player, from denim jeans to starched jodhpurs, from cowboy boots to polo mallets, all of which were inundating the advertising pages of magazines and daily newspapers, coincided with Vreeland's organization of "Man and the Horse." Lauren's celebration of upper-class horsemanship and apparel corresponded to Vreeland's preoccuption with what she called the "polo swells" of titled European social strata. Vreeland's museum vision of equestrian history and costume as a history of what she called "witticism, tradition, and high society far from urban rot" echoed Lauren's evocation of a world where stability, pedigree, and tradition infused life and costume with grace, beauty, and timeless style.

Diana Vreeland and Ralph Lauren's parallel affirmations of the privileged world of the thoroughbred and its exquisitely tailored society converged for a joint venture: Ralph Lauren agreed to become the single corporate sponsor for Vreeland's "Man and the Horse," donating $350,000 for the Met exhibition. Masterminded by the museum's chief fund-raiser, Emily K. Rafferty, the Lauren sponsorship was conceived as providing a perfect fit between the theme of the show and the "designer of Polo clothing for the horsey set and would-be horsey set." "It was the first thing that came to mind," stated Mrs. Rafferty as she described her selection of Lauren as a target for the horse-show financial sponsorship. Ralph Lauren indicated that he was personally asked to support the show by Diana Vreeland, a longtime acquaintance from the fashion world, and he remarked on his special interest in this particular Met exhibition:

> It represents a world I believe in, one that has been my inspiration for a long time. The show will give more people the chance to see the stylishness that came out of that world.

A mutually beneficial bargain was struck between the Met fund-raisers and Ralph Lauren. Under the new corporate sponsor's program, the Met, and Mrs. Rafferty in particular, had developed special skills in matching exhibitions with the "public image of potential sponsors," which often spilled over into corporate marketing aims. In return for the $350,000 grant, the Met agreed to affix Lauren's own name

and the sportswear logo, Polo, to all the publicity associated with the show, from poster to invitations to catalogue and postcards, as well as to the walls of the exhibition galleries. In addition, Lauren was granted the privilege of escorting Diana Vreeland to the annual Met party, the December benefit for the Costume Institute. Stung by intermittent criticism that his design work was "derivative" and less original than his fashion competitors, Lauren found in the Met benefit package a means for gaining an elevated entry into the elite circles of society and fashion design supporting the Costume Institute, as well as a way to enjoy the prestige of succeeding couturier Yves Saint Laurent as the featured living designer promoted in the museum's galleries.

The legitimation of wealth and the quest for cultural status, so perennial a theme in the connection between art museums and their benefactors, was transposed into a new key in the case of Ralph Lauren's association with the Met. Rather than donating art or funds for the arts under his own name in the traditional philanthropic pattern, Lauren underwrote a fashion show glorifying riding clothing and attached his company's Polo emblem to it. The visibility of Polo in the museum's costume galleries, and throughout the many Met gift-shop stations, could only enhance the sales of the multitude of products manufactured by the Lauren Polo empire. Indeed, the museum, filled with millions of visitors, accomplished a unique advertising feat. Lauren's "Man and the Horse" funding constituted an unusual and unchallenged advertising opportunity. Rather than having to compete and jostle with others in the pages of magazines for the attention of potential buyers, Lauren's Polo had the field to itself in the museum, fixed on the walls to be absorbed by the ever-replenishing crowds milling through the Costume Institute. In addition, there was an obvious linkage between the contents of "Man and the Horse" and the sources of the Lauren Polo design themes. Lauren treated the placard at the entry to "Man and the Horse," and the poster announcing and commemorating the show, in the same way he had treated his lavish photo advertising ensembles, combining image and signature to evoke privileged elites enjoying the company and sport of horses. Lauren's museum publicity boldly printed: *"Man and the Horse, presented by Polo/Ralph Lauren."* The poster for the Met show depicted a reproduction of a nineteenth-century painting of an English lord in riding habit, seated in one of many visible rooms of his country estate, gazing out at the beholder. Inscribed at his feet were lines of print announcing the Metropolitan Museum "Man and the Horse" exhibition and dates, "Presented by Polo/Ralph Lauren." The nineteenth-century painted portrait of nobility now replaced the photos of lanky men and women horse owners and riders posed, in Polo fashions, on the lawns and in the rooms of English country manors. The logo and signature on the ad ensembles, drawing the viewer into the landed gentry "life-style" through apparel, now beckoned the spectator into the museum history of elite equestrian garb. Many viewers, visually primed by months of Lauren Polo ads preceding the Met show, and confronted with vast Polo boutiques in large department stores, would have found it difficult to dissociate the images conjured up in Lauren's ads from the components and form of the Met exhibition. The museum galleries, filled with rows of male and female mannequins in riding habits, and surrounded by leather boots, canes, carved wood trunks, polo gear, and wool blankets, resembled diorama sets and props for Lauren's Polo images of the "Thoroughbred" line of home furnishings and Polo apparel, both inspired by the "timeless," "stylish" "way of living" of the world of elite equestrian sport and possession.

Next to the Saint Laurent show, the Met "Man and the Horse" exhibition was the most directly and unabashedly commercial of the suite of Vreeland's "historical" excursions. The "Eighteenth-Century Woman," funded by Merle Norman Cosmetics, and "La Belle Epoque," sponsored by Pierre Cardin, surely garnered certain benefits for their sponsors. But in these cases the contents of the shows were less explicitly linked to the sponsors' current merchandise, and the names and products of these companies were not as prominently displayed as was the Polo/Ralph Lauren emblem in the "Man and the Horse" show and everything connected with it. One room of the exhibit was devoted to the equipment and costume of the polo game, the favorite sport of English and Argentine aristocrats. Included were uniforms, headgear, mallets, boots, and special saddles. The Lauren symbol of mounted rider with raised mallet was now situated in the graphic details of the sportsman's illustrious historical setting.

While the "Man and the Horse" exhibition was the most visibly commercial of Vreeland's Met exhibitions, it was at the same time emphatically aristocratic, with a different focus than Vreeland's other projects of aristocratic idealization. In "Man and the Horse" Vreeland turned from a celebration of aristocratic ostentation, luxury, and conspicuous opulence to a glorification of the noble restraint, subtlety, and coded elegance represented by the tailored riding uniform. The stated emphasis of the new show was the discipline and correctness of the exclusive world of horsemanship, which was associated with the more traditional notion of aristocratic discretion rather than with the noble cult of hedonism stressed by Vreeland in the "Eighteenth-Century Woman" and "Belle Epoque" exhibitions. In an interview in *Vogue* on the origins and meaning of the new "Man and the Horse" show, Vreeland stated that she was interested in highlighting the strict *"exactness, precision,* and total correctness" of elite equestrian activity.

> There is no room for eccentricity in this world. . . . If you're looking for *chic,* turnout is the acme of perfection. But there is absolutely no room for incorrectness. Anywhere! And when is the last time you've seen something totally straight? I adore the maintenance of this world. Elegance is maintenance. . . . Luxury stands for nothing in the world of the horse. . . . Out cubbing with a pack, you first have respect for the horse, the others in the field, and especially for the correctness of it all.

The "perfection" and "correctness" of the world of the fox hunt, the polo match, the horse race, and the thoroughbred owner were reflected in the "Man and the Horse" display of riding apparel and their rigorously coded meanings. The exhibition confronted the viewer with galleries of mannequins in riding habits, whose color, cut of fabric, and number of brass-engraved jacket buttons indicated the precise rank of each of its wearers and the hunting society to which they belonged. The numerous galleries and commentary identified the continuity of quality and protocol in the world of elite man and the horse. Materials in the show that dated before the eighteenth century belonged to the tradition of royal and chivalric hunts and equestrian tournament sport, which dressed the riders and their horses in the distinctive colors and coats of arms of their lineage. This tradition was juxtaposed with its modern equivalents, the "racing silks of gentlemen jockeys," whose colors and symbols similarly represented their contemporary owners. The one element of transformation noted in the exhibition was the eighteenth-century invention of the "cutaway," a long-skirted riding coat cut away at the waist for the rider's greater ease of movement in the fox hunt. The cutaway replaced the elabo-

rately embroidered and brocaded long jackets worn by earlier generations of noblemen. Despite its apparent simplicity, it was wrought by
the most complex and exclusive tailoring and rigorously incorporated
the symbols of social distinction. Underscored in the Vreeland exhibition was the luxury not of external surface but of internal lining
within the sturdy, "exquisitely tailored" ensembles for elite horsemanship. Vreeland instructed the spectator in the elaborate codes and
strict discipline informing every aspect of the riding uniform and
accoutrements, which had operated, largely unchanged, since the
eighteenth-century invention of the cutaway. Shirts, breeches, jackets,
hats, and boots were strictly custom-made and conformed to the
highest standards of workmanship and were of the finest quality of
material. Vreeland's viewers were also informed about the small
number of sources in England and France where riding apparel and
riding boots can be custom-made to traditional standards. Sidesaddle
fox-hunting habits have issued for two centuries from the British
tailor Busvines, while leather boots, of rigorously monitored length,
are mainly supplied by the London specialty house of Peal & Company.
Thus the visible flourishes of detail, ornament, or "eccentricity" were
absolutely banished in the costumes of "Man and the Horse"; excel-
lence of fabric, quality of leathers, and strict adherence to a code of
rules testified to the superior status of the riding elite. Lavish external
luxury was apparent only in some of the accoutrements selected by
Vreeland, which resembled the artifacts of loaded surface display
monopolizing Vreeland's previous exhibitions. Typical of these elaborately decorated objects, which relieved the somewhat monotonous
array of monochrome riding habits, was a gold and silver sculptured
rococo saddle for the French king in the first gallery and the "Bavarian
state chariot used for transporting royalty" set adjacent to the model
tack room and polo room transforming the back gallery of the Costume
Institute.

Diana Vreeland's fascination with the etiquette and restraint of
the exclusive world of horsemanship extended the glorification of
aristocracies of blood and breeding and their equestrian companions
contained in *D.V.* Just as Ralph Lauren's customers were visually
prepared by Polo ads for the Met array of gentry mannequins in
riding apparel, so readers of *D.V.* were given a literary preparation for
Vreeland's particular conception of "man and the horse." Vreeland

described her lifelong "obsession with horses": "There is not a day in my life that I do not think about horses. On the hour, every hour." As a child, playing with toy horses and observing real horses "were all I cared about," noted Vreeland in *D.V.* This attitude seemed to be carried over into Vreeland's adult life. One of the only recorded expressions of emotional pain in *D.V.* is reserved for the death of a horse—a "terrible" event—which contrasts with the lack of registered discomfort at the numerous human deaths recounted in the memoir, including that of Vreeland's own husband.

D.V. associated the beloved horse with perfectly controlled and perfectly groomed nobility, displayed in the teams of suited riders drawing the royal coaches for the coronation of George V, which Vreeland claimed to have witnessed as a child. Elsewhere in *D.V.* the princely "polo swells" and the "grands seigneurs" paraded in their "cutaways and grey toppers." The Duke of Westminster was one of these aristocratic horsemen, who, the reader was informed, was named after Bendor, a horse who won the Derby. The duke's own exquisite breeding required him to "have his shoelaces ironed every day." Vreeland associated the beauty and perfection of the horse, and the dedication it inspired, with the qualities and inspirational force of women, who occupied the central spaces in all the previous shows. Both horse and woman functioned in Vreeland's rendering as at the disposal of, and in charge of, their male companions.

It was strange that Vreeland, whose previous museum projects had maximized the bizarre, the startlingly irregular, and the shockingly novel, should create an exhibition dedicated to the "totally straight" and to the world of "elegant maintenance," rigid protocol, and sartorial restraint. The concentration on dull gray and black riding habits, occasionally enlivened by colorful accessories, configured a stiff, uniform world whose only apparent claim on the spectator was as a voyeuristic entrée to the most exclusive of high society leisure activities and dress codes. "Man and the Horse" lacked the perverse panache and theatricality of Vreeland's earlier museum extravaganzas; by contrast, it was flat, monotonous, and uncompelling. One reason for the visual sterility of the show may have been the departure of Costume Institute curator Stella Blum, who was the indefatigable realizer of Vreeland's

Diana Vreeland rampant *(after David's portrait of Bonaparte),*
by Andy Warhol

earlier Met spectacles, and who held staff and scholars together in spite of Vreeland's erratic commands. Yet beyond this personnel factor, there was a broader thematic correspondence between the visual flatness of the show and the clarity of its commercial purpose. Despite the exhibit's appeal to hierarchy and aristocracy, it was a transparent and unlayered tribute to consumerism. The Lauren-Vreeland collaboration culminated the development of museum history as luxury commercial stimulant that had unfolded since the Met-Bloomingdale's China shows of 1982. Between 1981 and 1984 Vreeland's Met projects had become more and more unabashedly antihistorical and commercially laden. The "Chinese Robes," "Eighteenth-Century Woman," and "Belle Epoque" exhibitions had historical pretexts, although reshaped by Vreeland to conform to an image of elite extravagance, insulation, and irresponsibility resonant with the social beneficiaries of Reaganomics. The historical character of the Yves Saint Laurent "retrospective" was subordinated to a tribute to the living generations of the couturier's customers, who donated their outfits of years past to the show and then paraded in front of them in the new season's YSL ensembles.

"Man and the Horse" shed even the pretense of a historical account by reducing the museum display to an evocation of Polos past and a preview of Polo fashions to come. Vreeland's familiar technique of organizing exhibition components in nonchronological jumbles of surface juxtapositions worked to make "Man and the Horse" resemble the Lauren polo ads; there was no information or material to prevent the viewer from having this perception. Written accounts of the show confirmed this connection by noting, as *New York* magazine did, that the history of "Man and the Horse" revealed to the public the "birth of sportswear," for, it was claimed, the practical, stylish, casual American clothes we know as "sportswear" originated in the gentry cutaways of yesteryear featured in the museum.

The undisguised character of "Man and the Horse" as a specific catalyst for the immediate future of fashion design was also evident in the way the show was reviewed in the press. The *New York Times* celebrated the exhibition as "the most snobbish of all of Mrs. Vreeland's presentations" and as "enriching, enjoyable, and most satisfying." The "height of luxury" and "the precision of dress" featured at the

Ralph Lauren's 1985 equestrian fall fashion
(Alen MacWeeney © 1985; model: Frauke, Name Model Agency)

show were glorified precisely as having a powerful potential effect on designers' upcoming fall lines:

> It is . . . a show that may well leave its mark on any creative person worth his or her thread and needle, sketch pad or bolt of fabric. . . . Indeed, in deciding to mount this particular show at this time, when world fashion is at a creative standstill, Mrs. Vreeland is once again pointing the way ahead. . . . The "Man and the Horse" show at the Metropolitan Museum may well leave its mark on next fall's fashions. . . . It is easy to see why . . . this show may well have a lasting effect on today's designers, now just beginning to formulate their thoughts for next fall's collections. . . . So perhaps we should have a hunting horn salute to Mrs. Vreeland and the Metropolitan's Costume Institute, for mounting an educational and perhaps even prophetic show.

The "prophecy" of the show was not hard to predict, for within three months, as the fall 1985 fashions began to preview in the New York showrooms, it became clear that the Met had indeed "left its mark" on the emerging creations. Ralph Lauren's new line represented the closest fit between the outfits arrayed in the museum and his "inventions" for fall customers. His major ensemble, featured in the *New York Times Magazine* assessment of the fall collection, incorporated all the elements of the correct and elegant custom riding habit exhibited at the museum: high-necked, bright white silk chemise tied at the neck, sleek black breeches, black bowler hat, and red knitted jacket in the shape of the Paul Mellon red hunting habit featured in the Met show. Lauren's fall mannequin even held a stylish carved riding crop in her black-gloved hands, a direct copying of mannequins in the Vreeland exhibit. A second announcement of "fall dressing" again included Ralph Lauren's reproductions of the museum's equestrian outfits. Lauren's favored item for the 1985 fall preview was the "suede jodhpurs, with derby hats and bits of lace at the throat." The movement from consumer product to museum fabrication and back again could not have been any more explicit.

FIVE

THE THOROUGHBRED INAUGURATION

REAGANISM AND

VREELANDIAN CULTURE

1985

---

*Nancy Reagan represents what I would call a
thoroughbred American look: elegant,
affluent, a well-bred, chic American look. . . .
It's elegant, it's not overbearing . . . she has
expensive taste, but it's an image of good
taste.*

—Adolfo

n *D.V.* Diana Vreeland compared the beautiful and well-groomed
women she admired in the Paris Bois de Boulogne to the graceful
horses that transported them in open carriages to take the morning
air. Since the 1981 inauguration, admirers of the new First Lady
also invoked an equestrian comparison. Adolfo, one of Nancy
Reagan's favorite designers, represented Mrs. Reagan as the "American thoroughbred"—affluent, elegant, and impeccably groomed.
Tom Tierney, in *Nancy Reagan: Fashion Paper Dolls in Full Color*,
also associated Nancy Reagan's "distinctive look of quiet elegance"
with the classic "American thoroughbred," the model of "chic upper-
class style and breeding."

The exhibition of elite equestrian costume and traditions in the

Metropolitan Museum in the months preceding and following Ronald Reagan's second presidential term provided an interesting lens with which to view the inaugural festivities. There were striking affinities between the American "thoroughbreds" in the White House and the "thoroughbreds" featured at the museum, between the themes and style of the second Reagan inaugural and Vreeland's "Man and the

Horse" at the Met. The two public displays reinforced each other. The 1985 inaugural celebrations comprised a contradictory mixture of heightened social exclusivity, sartorial elegance, and media-commercial accessibility that paralleled Vreeland's composition of "Man and the Horse." Vreeland's 1981 glorification of the staggering surface splendor of Chinese imperial robes at the Met had coincided with the extravagant outburst of opulence characterizing the 1981 inauguration galas. The understated custom tailoring of high-society horsemanship at the Met in 1985 now resonated with the tempered "upper-class chic" distinguishing the second inaugural festivities. Yet, like the Polo/Lauren gentry that simulated history and tradition at the museum, the 1985 stylized noble discretion of the Reagan entourage was a flat, hollow façade, whose inauthenticity was as transparent as the Met "English" mannequins ubiquitously enveloped by the Polo/Lauren signature.

The Second Inauguration: Luxury Internalized and the Super Bowl

The 1985 Reagan inaugural planners did not want to repeat the excesses of the 1981 festivities. The unbridled visible luxury was considered both extreme and unnecessary in 1985. By December of 1984 presidential power and Republican leadership were fully consolidated, and the second time around, though lavish and expensive, the inaugural would symbolize the experience of control rather than the first flush of victory. And the tempered appearances of the 1985 inaugural galas would make it more difficult for the media to criticize the unchecked indulgences and glaring disparities noted in 1981.

Like the shift from glittering opulence to tailored luxury in Vreeland's museum treatment of privileged elites, the 1985 inaugural fetes moved from the opulent exteriority of 1981 to an interiorized, insulated luxury. Some effort was made to promote Inaugural '85 as a populist, simple affair. The official theme selected by the Presidential Inaugural Committee was "We the People: An American Celebration." John Buckley, committee spokesman, told the *New York Times* that "everything . . . will be less regal than in 1981." Numerous balls and receptions were offered to Republican youth and other groups at well below the thousand dollars a couple that was charged in 1981. Yet, as the *Washington Post* and the *New York Times* noted, a rigid division was established between the modestly priced parties and the events for the Reagan elite entourage. In 1985 the same group of people who had flocked to Washington in limousines, furs, and couture ensembles redescended upon Washington. Estée Lauder, Charles and Mary Jane Wick, William French and Jean Smith, Walter and Lee Annenberg, Frank Sinatra, Oscar de la Renta, Arnaud and Alexandra de Borchgrave, Bill Blass, Betsy Bloomingdale, and Jerry Zipkin spent their hours and displayed their clothes and jewels in private, exclusive receptions and evening balls to which the press was not invited. The public splendor of 1981 gave way to private luxury in 1985.

Nancy Reagan in particular sought in the 1985 inaugural to promote a new, refined, and tasteful image of herself as a dignified First Lady. She did not, as in the first inaugural, seek the limelight to exhibit her array of glittering outfits, jeweled custom-made shoes, embroidered handbags, and arm-length white gloves. The press was given a terse preview of Mrs. Reagan's outfits for the inaugural week, which included an "electric blue Adolfo suit," a "jeweled evening dress" studded with crystals by Galanos, a red suit for the private swearing-in ceremony, and a "red evening sheath designed by Bill Blass." On further checking, the *Washington Post* established that the quest for sartorial simplicity and tempered expense was inapplicable to Mrs. Reagan: for 1985, she nearly doubled her $25,000 wardrobe cost of 1981, spending $46,000 for the second-inaugural costumes. In 1985 Mrs. Reagan also continued to convey, according to *Time* magazine, an "ancien régime air" and to cultivate, as noted by a former aide, "an element of Louis XIV's French court and *les précieuses*—the affected ladies." And Mrs. Reagan's clique of close associates were present at events in the 1985 inaugural private galas that extended the social disparities publicly flaunted in 1981 and deepened the impression of unconsidered luxury amidst growing deprivation. The press followed Nancy Reagan's friends as they prepared their toilettes and coiffures for each evening's exclusive galas. Estée Lauder came to Washington loaded with suitcases filled with complete alternate wardrobes—one for warm and one for cold weather. One cold evening, she settled on a black velvet Saint Laurent gown and was considering, according to a *New York Times* reporter, "wearing a black jeweled veil." Echoes of the Vreeland Saint Laurent Met show with its mannequins in glittering face-veil stockings reverberated! Other press coverage of the inaugural ladies attending Nancy Reagan discussed the women's divided loyalties vis-à-vis hairdressers: as in 1981, Mrs. Reagan was still devoted to both Robin Weir, her Washington coiffeur, and Julius Bengtsson, her longtime Los Angeles stylist. Articles on the inaugural-week preparations showed Mrs. Reagan's entourage choosing between the two salons for their coiffures, and the kinds of services rendered in addition to the hairdos. Pat Buckley and Jerry Zipkin preferred Robin Weir, who served on-the-house omelettes and champagne to the clientele. Julius Bengtsson had the cachet of having accompanied Mrs. Reagan to Windsor Palace in 1982, and won the attention during inaugural week of Nancy's longtime close personal California friends Marion Jorgenson and Betty Wilson. Bengtsson was photographed in the salon "wearing suede shoes by Ralph Lauren, burgundy cord trousers by Calvin Klein, and a matching sweater by Gucci (a gift from Mrs. Wilson, whose husband was ambassador to the Vatican), topped with a jacket of beaver fur." Bengtsson exclaimed that he "loved Lauren/Polo" as he dashed to attend to Mrs. Reagan's hair before he himself got dressed to join the other honored guests for one of the private inaugural parties.

During the week of the descent of the socialites on Washington to celebrate four more years of the Reagans, public attention was directed to a report on poverty in New York released by the Community Service Society. In the findings of NYU economist Emmanuel Tobier, the effects of Reaganomics came through in stark relief. In 1979 one-third of New York city's children—552,000—lived below the poverty line. Tobier estimated that by 1982 the figure "had probably moved well over the forty-percent mark," and that by 1990 one out of every three New Yorkers will be living in poverty. Tobier pointed out that in the booming economy there was a widening gap between one prosperous segment of society and another segment marked by extreme poverty:

We are becoming a polarized, segmented city. While New York remains a city of gold for those at the top of the economic ladder, it has become a city of despair for many elderly, for the homeless, for women and children barely subsisting on public welfare.

To be sure, the Tobier report and commentaries on it did not blame the Reagan administration for causing poverty (the figures had been mounting over a long-term period since 1969). But the report and analysts isolated the Reagan administration's contribution to poverty escalation by the policies of cuts in social programs and welfare eligibility, and also noted the glaring contrast between the rhetoric of opportunity and enterprise and the reality of discouragement and unemployment. Writers discussing the Tobier report in *The New Yorker* noted that in 1969 a family of four with no earnings received welfare payments of 97 percent of the amount needed to raise it above the poverty line. In 1984 the same family could optimally receive only 60 percent of what it needed to move above the poverty line. Furthermore, the federally defined poverty-line figure for New York in 1984 was $10,200 for a family of four, which, as noted by Sydney Schanberg of the *New York Times*, is hardly "a survival income in this high cost city." The working poor and unemployed underclass have been ruthlessly cut off by the Reagan budget cuts, both from welfare and from job-training programs. Even the food program of the WIC (Women, Infants, and Children), used to improve the diet of malnourished pregnant and nursing mothers, was substantially reduced and required more stringent proof of eligibility.

The 1985 inauguration celebrations were organized to circumvent the confrontation of the worlds of opulence and disinheritance so embarrassingly apparent in 1981. The closed luxury parties and the populist youth fetes deflected attention from the underside of Reagan's "Opportunity Society." Yet in 1985, as in 1981, the stark divisions of an emerging contour of "two nations" surfaced, at least in the midst of the elite revelers. The French Revolution, which erupted after years of intensified and physically displayed gaps between the very rich and the very poor, was on the mind of Mrs. Pat Buckley, organizer of the Met Costume Institute galas launching each of Diana Vreeland exhibitions and a party-goer at the 1985 Washington celebrations. During the Met Yves Saint Laurent retrospective,

Mrs. Buckley gave an interview to Charlotte Curtis. She discussed the special vegetarian diet of Beep, her pet King Charles spaniel, and then commented, "I've never made the trip to or from Connecticut without its resembling the worst excesses of the French Revolution." A similar cast of analogical thinking was expressed at the inaugural fete itself by Mrs. Meese, whose husband was awaiting confirmation as attorney general despite a scandal involving huge interest-free loans and government appointments for the lenders. Considering her attendance at an inaugural pageant, Mrs. Meese alluded to Marie Antoinette. Her comment was quoted by John Duka of the *New York Times*:

> "You know, I've been having the best time," said Mrs. Meese. . . . "The prelude pageant was very exciting. The heat was turned up in the viewing box because Nancy gets cold. It got very hot, and for a moment I felt a little like Marie Antoinette." She moved her index finger across her neck.

The elevated aristocratic self-image of the Reagan elite at the 1985 inauguration was flattened by the realities of commercial interest and the ideology of self-creation, unanchored in stable family or social grouping. The gala inaugural events were sponsored by loans and donations totaling $9 million from large corporations, many of whose managers attended the presidential ceremonies. Hoping to be beneficiaries of the president's second term, as they had been of the first, were the corporate lenders of the largest sums in 1985: Hughes Aircraft, Rockwell International, and Martin Marietta, all major manufacturers of military products. President Reagan's postponing of the official swearing-in ceremony and parties from Sunday, January 20, to Monday, January 21, in order that he might appear as the official coin-tosser for the Super Bowl was also a departure from the theme of regal protocol and insulation.

The tawdry mixture of politics and show business, commercial interest and populist illusion, emerged in the planning and airing of a televised "50th Presidential Inaugural Gala," emceed by Frank Sinatra and funded by fourteen corporations spending $330,000 a minute in commercial time to pay for it. The preparations for the ABC TV gala were coordinated by Joseph Canzeri, public relations consultant, and former executive assistant to Michael Deaver. Canzeri had resigned from his official White House post in 1982 after it was disclosed that he had procured a $400,000 loan on unusually favorable terms. Out of the White House, Canzeri continued to work for his former boss as a media consultant. During the 1984 campaign he mobilized Frank Sinatra and Henry Kissinger for fund-raising efforts, and after the electoral victory accepted the chair of the inaugural gala committee. His organizational experience and talent for finding the compelling image shaped the televised gala of 1985. "Politics and entertainment are both perceptions," Canzeri stated in a press interview. With Vreelandian breeziness, he noted, "Don't confuse me with a lot of facts, just tell me what you want done."

For the January 19 ABC gala, what was wanted was a combination of royal tribute and patriotic celebration. As in the 1981 TV gala, the Reagans were constantly in camera view as they sat enthroned in winged chairs before a large stage, surveying the entertainment as if court jesters were on display. A glittering honor guard of Army, Navy, and Marine men flanked the seated couple, and blue carpeting, red theater seats, and white-draped ceilings created an American-flag effect. Symbolizing the theme "We the People: An American Celebration," the performers at the gala were of different races, party affiliations, and social strata. They ranged from Mr. T., Rich Little, and Elizabeth Taylor to Donna Summer and the dancing Breakers. Frank Sinatra had earlier in the week been angered by stories about the return of the Rat Pack to Washington and had told a reporter, "You are dead, all of you." But he was calmer as M.C., reemerging as the bland favorite of Mrs. Reagan, who regally dubbed him her "Francis Albert." The TV gala was a paltry and tiresome pageant. The Beach Boys appeared, dedicated "California Girl" to Nancy, and offered a final thanks to her for defending them against James Watt. Tom Selleck and Mr. T. made short speeches and were followed by an undignified Dean Martin, who joked about Reagan's victory as ushering in four more years of partying and alcohol imbibing. Elizabeth Taylor's announcement, now featured at the beginning of the Academy Award show, explained that the TV inaugural gala was to be beamed, via satellite, to the Eastern bloc nations, so that people all over the world could see the harmonious vision of the American people and their president. Ronald Reagan's longtime friend,

actor James Stewart, offered an interesting commentary on the old
Hollywood in a tribute to the presidential couple. Reminiscing,
Stewart said that the Hollywood that formed him and the Reagans
was "a magic place, where dreams were put on celluloid for all the
world to see," dreams of "patriotism and family."

Dreams into celluloid—Stewart's phrase aptly captured the strange,
jumbled, and flat images of American unity as a TV variety show, as
slice-of-life, where one of every type of American entertainer was
included. Celluloid dreams of patriotism and family hovered on the
screen, forming a hollow mirage and focusing on the ageless, eternally
young, and splendidly isolated presidential couple, whose inseparability
had been forcefully wrought by the exclusion of their own children
and stepchildren. Dreams into celluloid also carried a perplexing
meaning as Ronald Reagan concluded the TV inaugural gala by re-
playing a wartime Hollywood dream in an inappropriate context.
After thanking all the performers, the president recalled his own past
in Hollywood, when actors had often appeared gratis at benefits for
a worthy cause. He compared the performers' service at the 1985 TV
special to the work of Helen Hayes during World War II, when she
donated her time as a tribute to an "I Am an American Day" sponsored
by Roosevelt at the height of wartime sacrifice. In a burst of patriotic
zeal unleashed by the memory of that event of 1942, Reagan restated
Helen Hayes's declamation to the 120,000 people assembled in a
makeshift stadium. The president of the era of antisacrifice thereby
superimposed the altruistic, fighting American over the rapacious
economic competitor promoted by his policies of the 1980s. Quoting
Hayes's selection, he recited:

> "My country tis of thee
> Sweet land of liberty
> Of thee I sing.
> Land where my fathers died,
> Land of the Pilgrim's pride,
> From every mountainside
> Let freedom ring."

"Let freedom ring"—this, indeed, was the fundamental message of
Ronald Reagan as he began his second term of office. Freedom, for

him, had a powerful negative meaning: freedom *from* dependency, freedom *from* constraint, freedom *from* personal and social barriers impeding individual self-fulfillment, freedom *from* the presence and menace of communism. Freedom, for Reagan, was the freedom of economic man, whose freedom emerges, in the words of his inaugural address, as "we make the economy the engine of our dreams."

Reagan's vision intersects with the ethos of freedom promoted by Diana Vreeland in her reign at the Metropolitan Museum of Art, and in the values she espouses in *D.V.* It may be instructive to conclude by isolating two levels of convergence between Reaganism and Vreelandism, one emanating from Nancy Reagan and one issuing from the president. The first convergence has to do with self-fashioning and fashion opulence, and the second, with the erosion of history by wish and the effect of that erosion on the political arena.

The conjuncture of Nancy Reagan and Diana Vreeland contributed to a growing emphasis on female opulence in fashion design in the past five years. In 1981 fashion industry spokesmen expressed the hope that Nancy Reagan's lifelong involvement with expensive, elegant dress would stimulate the fashion industry and "create an upward trend in dressier clothes." Mollie Parnis, a designer for first ladies until Mrs. Reagan (who stuck to her preference for James Galanos, Adolfo, and Bill Blass), predicted in 1981 that Nancy Reagan was "going to have a great influence on fashion. She likes clothes, she entertains beautifully, she will be wearing the right thing at the right time, and it has to filter down." By 1985 fashion trends indeed revealed that "opulence was the new tradition," and lavish custom tailoring was firmly entrenched in the public eye as a symbol of "thoroughbred" femininity. The affluent clientele and visibility of Mrs. Reagan's preferred couturiers also expanded. Adolfo, whose knitted suits transformed Chanel's tailored Parisianism into upper-class American-matron classics, regained the limelight as his faithful customers were photographed constantly in their favorite Adolfo daywear. In 1981 his costumes were identified as "a good barometer of what fashion will be about for the next four years"; this, in effect, catapulted the sartorial preferences originating with Betsy Bloomingdale, who had introduced Nancy Reagan to Adolfo in 1976, to center stage at the White House. Mrs. Reagan had a seemingly endless supply of Adolfo suits, with their braided trim and matching silk chemises, and she and

The Adolfo Club:

Nancy Reagan;
Gladys Solomon;
Harriet Deutsch and
Lee Annenberg

(Guy DeLort/W)
(Amy Meadow/W)

Betsy Bloomingdale, Harriet Deutsch, Lee Annenberg, and Nancy Kissinger occasionally appeared at parties or fashion shows in the same Adolfo outfits. At Adolfo's 1983 spring show, for example, eleven women wore the same Adolfo "silk leaf-print dress with matching cardigan." Custom conformity was the essence of Nancy Reagan's tasteful but unimaginative and exclusive wardrobe, as epitomized by her membership in "the Adolfo Club."

Other purveyors of couturier opulence also benefited from Mrs. Reagan's attention. Oscar de la Renta's concentration on sartorial splendor deepened after 1981, and his elite clientele also expanded. De la Renta's showings through 1985 offered "shimmering embroideries" and gilded draperies befitting an exponent of "Living well is the best revenge." James Galanos's fashions similarly continued to promote the lavish, luxurious embellishing of surface splendor. His 1983 showing of fall sweaters, for example, featured "pearls, thickly encrusted on bodice of sleek black evening shift" and "thickly jeweled jackets" mixing "angora and cashmere with a pile as deep as fur." As his mannequins paraded through the Baroque Suite of the Plaza Hotel, the radiant Los Angeles couturier noted that "expensive clothes are here to stay. . . . They stand for luxury. There are people who want the best quality. I know how to give it to them." In 1985 Galanos's jeweled long evening dresses were featured at a banquet for the Council of Fashion Designers of America. The five-hundred-dollar-a-plate dinner, held in the main hall of the New York Public Library, brought together Bill Blass, Oscar de la Renta, Ralph Lauren, and Geoffrey Beene to honor Galanos and Diana Vreeland. Galanos received the council's award to a standing ovation, after a showing of his fall collection, which included jeweled evening dresses chosen by Nancy Reagan for the 1985 inaugural balls. Mrs. Reagan sent Galanos a telegram of love and congratulations, which was read at the banquet by Gloria Vanderbilt. A second standing ovation of the evening was reserved for Diana Vreeland, in tribute to her work of bringing fashion to the public through the Metropolitan Museum of Art. Mrs. Vreeland received her award from Oscar de la Renta, who lauded her "contribution to fashion as art," her "eye, her taste and enthusiasm."

The traceable influence of Nancy Reagan was complemented by the Diana Vreeland impact on the fashion industry. The "horsey look" of Ralph Lauren and his direct connection to the Met's "Man and the Horse" in 1985 was preceded by other instances of the formative effect of Vreeland's exhibitions on fashion designers. Yves Saint Laurent's couture business experienced a vigorous "forward movement" in 1984, certainly enhanced by the ten-month public viewing at the Metropolitan Museum. Couture House of Chanel's evening creations featured at American social events in 1984 and 1985 included a new line of dresses directly inspired by Watteau paintings—an extension of Vreeland's "Eighteenth-Century Woman" into a contemporary fashion equivalent. Similarly, some couture designers favored the reinvention of costumes celebrated at Vreeland's "Belle Epoque" exhibition. In August 1983 the couture collection spring previews were characterized by their "opulence and distinctly *belle époque* look." The "belle époque theme throughout" resulted from the concentration on the bustled gown and the adaptation of the 1890s corseted and bustled silhouettes of Vreeland's Met exhibition. The article on this 1983 infusion of Belle Epoque couture into contemporary fashion also noted the "luxurious fabrics and intricacy of design" that were favored by the vigorously expanding ranks of couture clients, as well as these clients' status as "women with a lot of leisure, a personal maid or two and limitless bank accounts." In 1985 another instance of Belle Epoque fashion was offered for the spring couture collection by Karl Lagerfeld for Chanel: a "bustle-backed ball gown and lace bolero," extending the reappearance of the fin-de-siècle forms among socialite couturiers and their customers.

The impact of Nancy Reagan and Diana Vreeland, themselves both products and masters of the world of the media, was not, however, limited to the exclusive arena of couture and its restricted, affluent clientele. Haute couture, like politics and museum education, is attached to commercial-consumerist underwriting. At the heart of couture is licensing; and Nancy Reagan's and Diana Vreeland's influence was also traceable in the seamless world of advertising images and ready-to-wear clothing. A year after the closing of the Met "Belle Epoque" exhibition, a new perfume and a new line of jewelry and leather goods were spawned under the rubric of Maxim's de Paris. Maxim's, the Belle Epoque Paris restaurant, had been bought by Pierre Cardin and reassembled, before its final relocation in New York, for the December 1982 Met gala launching Vreeland's "Belle Epoque"

Ungaro's Belle Epoque ball gown (Jean-Luc Huré/NYT PICTURES)

exhibition. The new perfume, in a black bottle decorated with a striking red Art Nouveau whiplash design, appeared in large advertisements that bore the same name and visual symbolism Vreeland had used in the "Belle Epoque" show. This movement from museum to advertising culminated in the use of the Galland painting of demimondaine solicitation at Maxim's featured at Vreeland's Met exhibition as a backdrop for the ads for leatherware and jewelry. Inscribed across a close-up of Galland's couple leaning on Maxim's bar was "Maxim's de Paris," along with the suggestion "Indulge yourself in its luxury." At the bottom of the page the ad continued: "Very European. Very sophisticated. Very necessary. Maxim's jewelry, belts, and personal leather goods for men, distributed exclusively in the U.S.A. by Swank, Inc."

This process of commercialization comprises more than the "filter-down" effect of Mrs. Reagan's fashion role and extends to a more complex interactive field. There is a mutually reinforcing connection between popular opulent fashion and the dual roles of White House Nancy Reagan on the one hand and the television fantasy of "Dynasty's" Krystle Carrington on the other. In the weekly evening show Krystle is the devoted wife of a rich and loving "entrepreneur," and her sartorial splendor, like Mrs. Reagan's, is presumed to be the natural physical expression of her husband's competitive success in the marketplace. "Dynasty" began programming during the week of the first Reagan inaugural, in 1981, and exploited the confusion between fantasy and reality by occasionally featuring recognizable political figures, such as Henry Kissinger and Gerald Ford, as guests at some of the extraordinarily lavish parties attended by the Carrington clan. "Dynasty" has been complemented by a new popular show, "Lifestyles of the Rich and Famous," which purports to tell true stories of the rich. "Dynasty" fashions, along with perfume, jewels, accessories, and lingerie, are now marketed as department-store signature items and advertised to consumers as a way to "share the luxury," "share the treasures," and "share the magic" of the Carrington characters' staggering riches by buying their imprint on objects of daily use and appearance. Bloomingdale's premiered the Dynasty Collection in November 1984, and had the cast of the series on hand to launch the new line. Interestingly, the cast members were not presented as actors, but were introduced as if they really *were* the people they

*A gracious lifestyle of
elegant perfection.
A fantasy-come-true
world where that one
true love has waited,
and become...the love
that lives forever.
Welcome to Dynasty,
the world's most popular TV series. Now share
with us The Dynasty Collections and create your
very own reality.*

played on the show. Huge Bloomingdale's ads in the newspapers exclaimed, "Share today in the Magic of Dynasty. Meet Krystle Carrington, her family, friends and foes in person today from noon till 1." The copy continued, next to a photo of the devoted couple, Blake and Krystle Carrington:

> A gracious lifestyle of elegant perfection. A fantasy-come-true world where that one true love has waited, and become . . . the love that lives forever. Welcome to Dynasty, the world's most popular TV series. Now share with us The Dynasty Collection and *create your very own reality*.*

The world Vreeland created in *D.V.*, a world "as you feel it to be, as you wish it to be, as you wish it into being" reverberates here. And Ron and Nancy, embracing across the cover of and inside the June 1985 *Vanity Fair*, provide the pendant image of perfect, timeless romance to the Carringtons of Denver and Bloomingdale's.

"Create your very own reality," a standard advertising motto, not only applied to the way the public emulated the "Dynasty" life-style by buying commercial reproductions of its accoutrements. The appeal to "dreams come true"—meaning luxuriant wealth and true love—is one basis for the remarkable success of Ronald Reagan, who taps "Dynasty" themes in ordinary Americans' imaginations. It is the inundation of the political arena by wish-fulfillment that distinguishes the ideology and actions of Ronald Reagan. And this powerful political impetus to replace reality with fantasy renders Vreeland's dissolution of history in the cultural world more disturbing and significant.

Reagan's second inaugural sounded the theme of the infinite possibilities waiting to be seized by bold, individual dreamers once they were freed of all external barriers. The past was cited as one of these illegitimate barriers. Reagan identified history as an unwelcome brake on the present, and he advocated a "new beginning" for Americans, whose glory comes, "not from looking to the past," "not in looking backward," but in positioning for "a better tomorrow" that is "always" unfolding in "this blessed land." The simple formula for a

---

* Author's emphasis.

(Jules Feiffer. Copyright © 1985 Universal Press Syndicate.
Reprinted with permission. All rights reserved)

new beginning in 1985 was: "There are no limits to growth and human progress when men and women are free to follow their dreams." The dreams envisioned were made up of limitless personal riches; justice and ethical or social goals were banished from mention in a universe where the isolated risk taker was the ideal actor. In his 1985 inaugural address, Reagan, unlike Kennedy and Carter, offered everything without expecting anything in return; bringing to mind the dénouements of 1940s Hollywood movies, the president promised a happy ending, no matter what had happened in the interim. This was the magic of a world without pain, without sacrifice, without process, a world bulging only with pleasure and bounty for the takers. Ronald Reagan's inaugural speech propounded a "reality" like Diana Vreeland's—"as you feel it to be, as you wish it to be, as you wish it into being."

Reagan's promotion of fantasies of abundance and infinite self-fashioning intensified in his major speeches of the first months of his second term. The 1985 State of the Union message rang loud and clear in tribute to the rootless, unlocated individual, constrained only by the dreams and plans of his own making:

There are no constraints on the human mind, no walls around the human spirit, no barriers to our progress except those we ourselves erect.

In glorification of this free human spirit, Reagan selected two women as "American heroes" worthy of national recognition: Jean Nguyen, a Vietnamese refugee who came to the United States ten years ago and is now graduating from West Point, and seventy-nine-year-old Mother Hale of Harlem, who in Reagan's words, "lives in the inner city where she cares for infants born of mothers who are heroin addicts." The two women flanked Mrs. Reagan in the viewing booth, and the First Lady's glaring red dress and remote expression provided the greatest possible distance between her and the two heroines on either side of her. The president, pursuing his wonted style of bending and ignoring facts, obliterated the reasons why young Jean Nguyen arrived in the United States as a refugee from Saigon, and glided past the irony that Mother Hale's inner-city clinic was one of many social centers whose resources had been deeply cut by his own policies. He buoyantly hailed the two women as living representatives of "the oldest American saying—anything is possible if we have the faith, the will and the heart." "Great dreams," he concluded, "are dreams we can make come true."

In *D.V.* Diana Vreeland recounted how she defended herself when her grandson berated her for "lying so much," for "always telling the goddamnedest stories." Vreeland explained that there was a crucial difference between *deliberate* lying and embellishing or ignoring details "to make a good story." The latter, according to Vreeland, is not lying: "Some people *really believe* the lies they tell; they *believe* it all as they speak. It *grows* as they speak." This earnest endeavor is "romantic"—"lies to make life more interesting."

Ronald Reagan is one of those "who *really believe*" the stories they tell, and, like Vreeland, he does not deny facts, but willfully replaces them with fantasy. Reagan *believes*, as he stated in a speech at St. John's University, that "we have lived through the age of big industry and the age of the giant corporation" and are entering "the age of the entrepreneur, the age of the individual." Reagan *believes* that "we make dreams come true," that "there is always another tomorrow," and that "there are no limits when men and women are free to follow their dreams." Reagan recites and reenacts the triumph of The Gipper and offers the promise of success, if not success itself, to all Americans. Like Vreeland's, Reagan's own personal success is based on his playing fast and loose with the facts, on his "lifelong habit for exaggerating." As Laurence Leamer writes, "Though Dutch Reagan was brought up to tell the truth, he believed facts were flat little balloons that had to be blown up to be seen and sufficiently appreciated." Yet Reagan's commitment to the real as "he wishes it to be, as he wishes it into being" has a more sinister side, beginning with his belief that Communists had infiltrated and directed the TVA, which led to his dismissal as host of the "General Electric Theater" in 1958. Since he became president, the underside of Reagan's immersion in reality as wish and his willful ignorance of history have been amply expressed, with devastating consequences: the espousal of Star Wars; the proposition that "the Contras are the moral equals of our Founding Fathers"; the statement that "most Americans are of the opinion that the members of the Lincoln Brigade were fighting on the wrong side"; the collapsing of widely divergent forms of political extremism into a single international branch of Murder, Inc.; and the Bitburg fiasco, during which the president delivered himself of one outrageously antihistorical and morally grating proclamation after another. These ranged from Reagan's initial statement that most Germans who had experienced the war were no longer alive, to the tale, drawn from *Reader's Digest* and recounted at the Bitburg Air Base, of a peaceful Christmas dinner shared by German and American teenage soldiers "in a small cottage in the woods" during the Battle of the Bulge, to, finally, the suggestion that German soldiers were mainly young victims of one man's evil totalitarian rule, just as concentration-camp inmates were victims. Such a jumble of illusions is as difficult to absorb now as it was when the Bitburg incident first unfolded.

The themes of opulence, privilege, and historical fantasy were amply extended across a spectrum of American culture in 1985. Diana Vreeland prepared her new Metropolitan Museum exhibition, "Costumes of Royal India," a spectacle of India under the British Raj. Leaving behind the image of sartorial restraint and exclusive uniformity befitting the landed gentry of the "Man and the Horse" show, Vreeland returned to a demonstration of overwhelming luxury and surface splendor such as had characterized her previous aristocratic fashion histories. Vreeland commented on the India exhibit in the following manner:

> That much wealth isn't luxury, it's unbelievable; A gold and silver bed! I mean what holds the box spring, what stands on the floor! Our shows have always been highly polished, but we have four polishers down there now, working on this one!

Royal India was accompanied by an extraordinary outburst of enthusiasm for its colonizer, Royal England. Ralph Lauren's admiration for English "aristocratic demeanor" and longstanding elite traditions was amplified by a national tribute to the landed nobilities of Great Britain and to the English royal couple, Prince Charles and Princess Diana. In November of 1985, the Washington National Gallery opened the largest art show it had ever mounted, "Treasure Houses of Britain: Five Hundred Years of Private Patronage and Art Collecting." In preparation for the exhibition, Director J. Carter Brown arranged not only for the inclusion of over six hundred art objects scattered throughout Great Britain but for the transportation to Washington of a large segment of the English aristocracy who owned the country houses whose collections were on display. During the first week of November, Washington society was overtaken by Anglomania and "royal fever," as individuals vied to articulate the correct forms of address and to curtsy before the likes of the Duke and Duchess of Marlborough, Lord and Lady Romsey, Lord Montagu, and the Marquess of Tavistock. Gala parties honoring the British lords and ladies featured many members of the Reagans' inner social circle, who had last assembled in Washington for the private parties of the second inauguration.

One week after the celebration of the opening of "Treasure Houses of Britain," with their illustrious owners presiding, Prince Charles and Princess Diana arrived in Washington. Their purpose was to see something of America, to visit the Reagans, and to promote British exports—both the elite museum version in the National Gallery exhibit and the commercial "knock-offs" of the British style featured at J. C. Penney's "Best of Britain" theme show. The Reagans sponsored a small private dinner party for the royal couple, which excluded most political officials such as the vice-president and the diplomatic corps in favor of a combination of Hollywood celebrities—Clint Eastwood, John Travolta, Tom Selleck—and Nancy's coterie—Betsy Bloomingdale, Lee Annenberg, Jerry Zipkin, and decorator Ted Graber. The evening, touted as the year's "most exclusive social event," was described by Betsy Bloomingdale as "the top of the social tree—you can't go any higher." Lee Annenberg, marveling at the sight of a young princess dancing in the arms of a handsome movie star, exclaimed that this was "one of the most exciting nights in the history of the White House." Princess Diana charmed all of Washington with her demure smile and lavish costumes, while the prince participated in a meeting with scholars to discuss and refurbish the reputation of his favorite ancestor, George III, against whom Americans rebelled in 1776.

The main attraction in the Washington tribute to England, "Treasure Houses of Britain" drew large crowds to a massive demonstration of aristocratic luxury and acquisitiveness. Critics pointed out that the show was less a historical examination of noble collections than a highly emotional glorification of the country-house owners. The catalogue and guide to the exhibit presented a one-dimensional, idealized image of the aristocracy as characterized by "humanity and cultivation, scholarship and lack of pomposity." Historians such as David Cannadine explained that this presentation of the nobility as the natural guardians of taste and the protectors of the national patrimony was "as historically unconvincing as it was politically backward," and that the exhibit was "not so much history as myth, in which there is no room (and no need) for dissent or a different point of view." Cannadine and others explained that the show underemphasized the startling range in the quality of aristocratic collections; the fact that the great landowners were not necessarily the most enlightened patrons of the arts; and that it was the houses themselves, rather than the arts they contained, on which the elite lavished their money and attention: the estates were "machines of power" and symbols of hierarchy, exclusiveness, and inequality.

British observers commenting on the Washington exhibition indicated that one purpose of the show was to promote the goals of the

Country House Lobby. The celebration of the total country house as a national treasure served to undermine the campaign, favored by some in England, to dismantle the art collections from the estates and disperse them to public trusts or museums. There was little explanation by American reviewers as to why there was such a fascination, on this side of the Atlantic, with the "snobbism and nostalgia" represented by the exhibit. Luxury and a staggering assemblage of what Lauren called "the atmosphere of the good life" were designed to limit viewers' critical judgment and curiosity.

There have been other times in our past marked by a contraction of the nation's conscience, by the substitution of profits for ethics, by the distrust of historical memory. The Gilded Age with which we began our discussion was such a period. Henry Cabot Lodge's warning in 1895 that "the darkest sign of the age is the way in which money and the acquisition of money seems rampant in every portion of the community" has striking resonance with themes in our society today, though these have different scope, intensity, and sources. That the center of politics and the centers of high culture glorify opulent wealth and fantasy as truth are dark signs of our age, which encourage a flight from reality and the erosion of compassion.

WORKS CONSULTED

PREFACE

Buckley, William F., Jr. "The Way They Are: Ron and Nancy Reagan." *Vanity Fair*, June 1985, pp. 49–53.

Carter, Paul A. *The Twenties in America*. 2nd ed. Arlington Heights, Ill.: AHM Publishing, 1975.

Dallek, Robert. *Ronald Reagan: The Politics of Symbolism*. Cambridge: Harvard University Press, 1984.

Goldsmith, Barbara. "The Meaning of Celebrity." *New York Times Magazine*, December 4, 1983, pp. 74–82, 120.

Hobsbawm, Eric, and Terry Ranger, eds. *The Invention of Tradition*. New York and Cambridge: Cambridge University Press, 1983.

Kidwell, Claudia, and Margaret Christman. *Suiting Everyone: The Democratization of Clothing in America*. Washington, D.C.: Smithsonian Institution Press, 1974.

Leach, William. "Gender and Consumption: 1870–1925." Paper prepared for Smith-Smithsonian Conference on the Conventions of Gender, February 16–17, 1984.

Lears, T. J. Jackson. *No Place of Grace: Anti-Modernism and the Transformation of American Culture, 1880–1920*. New York: Pantheon Books, 1981.

Lewis, Anthony. *Abroad at Home, New York Times*. "Ten Blind Meese," March 26, 1984; "The One-Track Mind," May 9, 1985; "War Is Peace," May 18, 1985.

Lowenthal, Leo. "Biography in Public Magazines," in P. Lazarsfeld and Frank N. Stanton, eds., *Radio Research, 1942–1943*, pp. 507–48. New York: Duell, Sloan & Pearce, 1944.

Rogin, Michael. "Kiss Me Deadly: Motherhood, Communism, and Cold War Movies," *Representations* 6 (Spring 1984):1–37.

Schickel, Richard. *Intimate Strangers: The Culture of Celebrity*. New York: Doubleday, 1985.

INTRODUCTION

Bing, S. "Artistic America." In *Artistic America, Tiffany Glass, and Art Nouveau*, translated by Benita Eisler, pp. 11–192. Cambridge: MIT Press, 1970. Originally published 1895.

Davis, John H. *The Kennedys: Dynasty and Disaster, 1848–1983*. New York: McGraw-Hill, 1984.

Harris, Neil. *The Artist in American Society: The Formative Years, 1790–1860*. New York: Braziller, 1966.

———. "The Gilded Age Revisited: Boston and the Museum Movement." *American Quarterly* 14/4 (Winter 1982):545–66.

Hobsbawm, Eric, and Terry Ranger, eds. *The Invention of Tradition*. New York and Cambridge: Cambridge University Press, 1983.

Horowitz, Helen Lefkowitz. *Culture and the City: Cultural Philanthropy in Chicago from the 1880s to 1917*. Lexington: University Press of Kentucky, 1976.

Howe, Winifred E. *A History of the Metropolitan Museum of Art*. New York: Gilliss Press, 1913.

Kouwenhoven, John A. *Made in America: The Arts in Modern Civilization*. Garden City, N.Y.: Doubleday, 1948.

Mumford, Lewis. *The Brown Decades: A Study of the Arts in America, 1865–1895*. New York: Harcourt Brace, 1931.

Roberts, Robert R. "Gilt, Gingerbread, and Realism: The Public Taste." In H. Wayne Morgan, ed., *The Gilded Age: A Reappraisal*, pp. 169–95. Syracuse, N.Y.: Syracuse University Press, 1963.

Saisselin, Rémy G. *The Bourgeois and the Bibelot*. New Brunswick, N.J.: Rutgers University Press, 1984.

Silverman, Debora. "Eclecticism, Modernism, Social Darwinism, and Materialism: The San Francisco World's Fair 1915." *Design Book Review*, Winter 1985, pp. 2–8.

Tipple, John. "The Robber Barons in the Gilded Age: Entrepreneur or Iconoclast." In H. Wayne Morgan, *The Gilded Age: A Reappraisal*, pp. 14–37.

Tomkins, Calvin. *Merchants and Masterpieces: The Story of the Metropolitan Museum of Art*. New York: E. P. Dutton, 1970.

Wharton, Edith, and Ogden Codman. *The Decoration of Houses*. New York: W. W. Norton, 1978. Originally published 1897.

CHAPTER ONE. CHINA AT BLOOMINGDALE'S
AND THE MET, 1980–1981

Bloomingdale's. "China: Heralding the Dawn of a New Era." Bloomingdale's Promotional Literature, September–December 1980.

Kornbluth, Jesse. "The Empress of Clothes." *New York*, November 29, 1982, pp. 30–36.

Leamer, Laurence. *Make-Believe: The Story of Nancy and Ronald Reagan*. New York: Harper & Row, 1983.

Metropolitan Museum of Art. *The Manchu Dragon: Costumes of China, the Ch'ing Dynasty, 1644–1912*. New York: Metropolitan Museum of Art, 1980.

Schell, Orville. *To Get Rich Is Glorious: China in the 80s*. New York: Pantheon Books, 1984.

Stanfill, Francesca. "Living Well Is Still the Best Revenge." *New York Times Magazine*, December 21, 1980, pp. 20–25, 56, 68–69, 74–76.

Vidal, Gore. "The Best Years of Our Lives," review of Laurence Leamer's *Make-Believe*. *New York Review of Books*, September 28, 1983, pp. 28–32.

Vreeland, Diana. *Allure*. Garden City, N.Y.: Doubleday, 1980.

CHAPTER TWO. FABRICATION AND FRANCOPHILIA:
THE FÊTES DE FRANCE AT THE MET AND
BLOOMINGDALE'S, 1981–1984

Bernier, Olivier. *The Eighteenth-Century Woman*. Garden City, N.Y.: Doubleday, New York, published in association with the Metropolitan Museum of Art, 1982.

Bloomingdale's. "Fête de France: A Dazzling Salute to the Products and Culture of France, Fall, 1983." *Supplement to the New York Times*, September 9, 1983.

Buck, Joan Juliet. "Yves Saint Laurent on Style, Passion and Beauty." *Vogue*, December 1983, pp. 298–301, 397.

Darnton, Robert. *The Great Cat Massacre and Other Episodes in French Cultural History*. New York: Basic Books, 1984.

Dionne, E. J. "A Salute to Yves Saint Laurent: The Man behind the Mystique." *New York Times Magazine*, December 4, 1983, pp. 160–64, 172.

Duffy, Martha. "Toasting Saint Laurent. A New York Retrospective Revels in Glamor and Luxury." *Time*, December 12, 1983, pp. 96–98.

Elias, Norbert. *The Court Society.* Translated by Edmund Jephcott. New York: Pantheon Books, 1983.

Ellenberger, Henri. *The Discovery of the Unconscious: The History and Evolution of Dynamic Psychiatry.* New York: Basic Books, 1970.

Filler, Martin. "The Taste of Power: Upstairs with Nancy and Ronnie." *Skyline*, March 1982, pp. 24–26.

Garner, Philippe. *Emile Gallé.* London: Academy, 1976.

Hufton, Olwen. *The Poor in Eighteenth-Century France.* New York: Oxford University Press, 1976.

Kimball, Fiske. *The Creation of the Rococo Decorative Style.* New York: Dover, 1980.

Metropolitan Museum of Art. *The Eighteenth-Century Woman.* New York: Metropolitan Museum of Art, 1981.

———. *La Belle Epoque.* New York: Metropolitan Museum of Art, 1982.

———. *Yves Saint Laurent.* New York: Clarkson Potter, 1983.

Nye, Robert. *Crime, Madness and Politics in Modern France: The Medical Concept of National Decline.* Princeton, N.J.: Princeton University Press, 1984.

Pear, Robert. "True Hunger and Malnutrition Cases Are Growing Problems, Experts Say." *New York Times*, December 19, 1983, p. 14.

Richardson, John. "Yves Saint Laurent's Château Gabriel: A Passion for Style." *Vogue*, December 1983, pp. 302–16.

Saint Laurent, Yves. "All about Yves: YSL on YSL." *New York*, November 28, 1983, pp. 50–55.

Uzanne, Octave. *Nos Contemporaines, les femmes à Paris.* Paris: Quantin, 1893.

CHAPTER THREE. D.V., THE BESTSELLER: "SNIFFING OUT SOCIETY" AND SELF-FASHIONING, 1984

Kombluth, Jesse. "The Empress of Clothes," *New York*, November 29, 1982, pp. 30–36.

Vreeland, Diana. *D.V.* Edited by George Plimpton and Christopher Hemphill. New York: Alfred A. Knopf, 1984.

CHAPTER FOUR. ''SPIT AND POLISH AND GREAT TAILORING'': MAN, THE HORSE, AND RALPH LAUREN'S POLO AT THE MET, 1984–1985

Diamonstein, Barbara Lee. "Ralph Lauren." *New York,* October 21, 1985, pp. 40–47.

Donovan, Carrie. "An Exhibit that Rides High." *New York Times Magazine,* January 20, 1985, pp. 54–56.

———. "Fashion Preview, New York Aims for the Top." *New York Times Magazine,* April 21, 1985, pp. 83–90.

Ferretti, Fred. "The Business of Being Ralph Lauren." *New York Times Magazine,* September 18, 1983, pp. 112–14, 124–25, 132–33.

Geist, William. "Three Purveyors of Executive Style." *New York Times Magazine,* Men's Fashions of the Times, September 8, 1985, pp. 78, 100.

Goodman, Wendy. "Man and the Horse: Diana Vreeland's Latest Costume Extravaganza." *New York,* November 26, 1984, pp. 65–72.

McGill, Douglas. "Art World Subtly Shifts to Corporate Patronage." *New York Times,* February 5, 1985.

Metropolitan Museum of Art. *Man and the Horse.* New York: Metropolitan Museum of Art, 1984.

Morris, Bernadine. "Trends in Fall Dressing: Wool Jersey Is a Favorite." *New York Times,* May 14, 1985, B6.

Salmans, Sandra. "The Fine Art of Museum Fund Raising." *New York Times,* January 14, 1985, D1, D3.

Talley, André Leon. "Bridled Passion." *Vogue,* December 1984, pp. 358–59, 404–405.

CHAPTER FIVE. THE THOROUGHBRED INAUGURATION: REAGANISM AND VREELANDIAN CULTURE, 1985

"Adolfo: The Elf of Fashion." *W,* October 19–26, 1984, pp. 14–15.

Andersen, Kurt. "Co-Starring at the White House, Nancy Reagan's Growing Role." *Time,* January 14, 1985, pp. 25–35.

Cannadine, David. "Brideshead Re-Revisited." *New York Review of Books,* December 19, 1985, pp. 17–22.

Cuniberti, Betty. "Royal Fever Has Them Reeling on the Potomac." *Los Angeles Times,* November 4, 1985, v, 1, 3.

Curtis, Charlotte. "Pat Buckley's Benefits." *New York Times,* November 20, 1984, C16.

Desai, Anita. "The Rage for the Raj." *New Republic*, November 25, 1985, pp. 26–30.

Donovan, Carrie. "Couture Carries On." *New York Times Magazine*, February 24, 1985, p. 67.

Duka, John. "In the Capital, Parties Break Out in Song." *New York Times*, January 21, 1985, A18.

———. "The Inaugural Look '85: Opulence Is Still in Fashion." *New York Times*, January 22, 1985, C12.

Gailey, Phil. "The Impresario of the Inaugural Galas." *New York Times*, January 17, 1985, A20.

Gamarekian, Barbara. "Hairdos and Champagne before the Century." *New York Times*, January 21, 1985, A18.

Hughes, Robert. "Brideshead Redecorated." *Time*, November 11, 1985, pp. 64–65.

Kaplan, Peter, "Why the Rich Rule the TV Roost." *New York Times*, April 7, 1985, 1, 29.

Leamer, Laurence. *Make-Believe: The Story of Nancy and Ronald Reagan*. New York: Harper & Row, 1983.

Lewis, Anthony. "The Two Nations." *New York Times*, April 4, 1985, A31.

Morris, Bernadine. "Bravos for Galanos' Sweaters." *New York Times*, August 17, 1983, C12.

———. "Couture Flourishes with Opulent Designs." *New York Times*, August 2, 1983, B4.

———. "A Toast to American Fashion." *New York Times*, January 15, 1985, B8.

Reagan, Ronald. Second Inaugural Address. Reprinted in *New York Times*, January 22, 1985.

———. 1985 State of the Union Address. Reprinted in *New York Times*, February 7, 1985.

Schanberg, Sydney. "The Poverty Divide." *New York Times*, January 22, 1985, op. ed. page.

"Talk of the Town." *The New Yorker*, April 1, 1985, pp. 29–30.

INDEX

ABOUT THE AUTHOR

Debora Silverman teaches European cultural history at the University of California, Los Angeles. She received her B.A., M.A., and Ph.D. from Princeton University. Her book on art, politics and psychiatry in fin-de-siècle France will be published by the University of California Press. She, her husband, and their son live in Los Angeles.